# Laughing Kitbags

Ian Ditch

*AuthorHouse™ UK Ltd.*
*500 Avebury Boulevard*
*Central Milton Keynes, MK9 2BE*
*www.authorhouse.co.uk*
*Phone: 08001974150*

*First published by AuthorHouse 4/20/2010*

*ISBN: 978-1-4490-7107-3 (sc)*

*This book is printed on acid-free paper.*

# PREFACE:

**"Laughing Kitbags"**: A Naval/Royal Marine saying meaning: To laugh heartily until you cannot laugh anymore. The type of laughter that leaves you finding it hard to even breathe! Enough laughter to fill a kitbag.

This book has been written because so, so many people have asked me to do it…..to the stage where I thought ` Christ…….. Lets get it done just to shut them up`!

Well, here it is!

It is dedicated to all those of whom I served with throughout my 23 years in the Royal Navy (F.A.A.) for they are the backbone of the dit`s you are about to read.

It is also dedicated to my late father Stan Ditch (ex stoker) and to Kenny Merritt (ex F.A.A.) to whom both I listened to as a lad when they had a `good dit` to tell.

Read on……………………………….....................................……

# ABOUT THE BOOK

The manuscript is a collection of some of the antics which the Author and his comrades got up to in the early stages of their naval careers. The Author has a no nonsense approach to narration telling it like it was with his own inimical style, trying his hardest to have the reader think they were there at the time. He has a gift for bringing to life the madcap characters and the uproarious pranks that made his own naval career so memorable. The Author sets out to make us laugh and this he does with his own particular brand of panache. On that note: some of the accounts are definitely adult fayre but anyone with a decent sense of humour should get a kitbag full of laughs out of it.

50p will be donated to Helpforheros by the Author for every copy of this book sold.

# BABIES HEADS & THE MAD DRUMMER

Dear readers……..

Who the hell is……. RICHARD M?

It was early 1981 and 846 Squadron helicopters are to embark onto the aircraft carrier HMS Bulwark, for it to sail us up to Norway where we would fly off and take part in a NATO exercise called `Teamwork`. We were put into Eagle Base groups and given our orders for the said exercise. An `Eagle Base` consisted of 1 helicopter, 3 aircrew, about 8 engineers, various equipment for field conditions, weapons, food, stores and a 12 man tent! Off we flew in our helicopters all loaded up, ready to take part in the exercise that had already started. Our pilot for this `dit` will be named….Lieutenant Branston-Pickle (to keep him out of the poo!). He really couldn't give `a toss` about anything and was using the Forces as a pass time as `mama and papa` were apparently loaded with money and so flying helicopters was just fun to him!

We were given the area we had to fly to which was a very large hill about 5 miles inland from where the ship had anchored. The hill was ideal, as all `8 Eagle Bases` could operate from there without being too close to one-another. We flew off the ship in tactical formation and made for our destination. On reaching the said hill, helicopters were landing in strategic places and would be starting to set up there base for the next 3 weeks. We flew on around the far side of the hill.

Lt. Branston-Pickle was looking out for somewhere where we could use the best natural cover and to blend in with the landscape. At the foot of the hill was a Norwegian farmhouse with outbuildings.

"That looks like just the spot for us" said Lt B-P and with that, started to descend.

As we landed and shut the helicopter down we saw the owner leaving his house and making his way towards us.

After the initial greetings were exchanged it had been decided that this was to be our operating area for the exercise for the next 3 weeks......Lt Branston-Pickle could speak fluent Norwegian and the farmer was delighted that he could be of some help to us. We unloaded the helicopter of all our stores and equipment and then the Aircrew flew off to the HQ to inform them of our position and receive their orders for the exercise. We started erecting our tent when the farmer (who was watching us) made a gesture that there was no need to do this and pointed to one of the outbuildings. We followed him into this building and realised that it was where he kept his cattle in the winter. Making a gesture that we sleep in here, he started sweeping the place out and so we happily gave him a hand.

"Better than a tent any day this eh"? Says Bob. "Too right mate, I think we might do alright here" I replied.

We soon had the place sorted and piled our field equipment and tent in a corner of the building. All the time the farmer was gibbering away in Norwegian, we just acknowledged him with a smile and stood around waiting for our cab to come back.

Whilst waiting, his wife came down from the house to see us with a tray of waffles and jam and a pot of coffee. Their children were with her. A boy of about 5, a girl of about 8 and a baby no older than say...4 months. Chatting away to us in Norwegian (thinking we understood them) while we enjoyed our waffles and coffee.

"Here he comes" says one of the fellas and with that, Lt Branston-Pickle comes hammering over the tree tops at about 50 foot, flies to the end of the tree line and then pulls the cab straight up in the air and does a `wing-over turn` then flies to where we are stood, comes to the hover and lands! Our Norwegian farmer and his family are loving this.....clapping as Lt. B-P gets out of the cab and joins us for coffee!

We stood having a smoke as he spoke to our hosts as though he was a local himself.

"OK chaps, this is what's happening" he said.

"HQ are happy with us staying here and said that....

`what a good idea it was blending in with the area`
and so we don't have to hang camouflage nets from the damn helicopter.   What they don't know though, is that we are staying in a building and they certainly don't know we have a friendly farmer and his family who wants to look after us.   The farmer has told me that we are welcome to use his house whenever we want but I've said that won't be necessary as we have everything with us".

"OK boss but what about using his loo at least eh, It's going to be better than squatting your arse over a hole that we are going to have to dig and then fill in afterwards eh"? I suggested.

"OK, toilets OK, yes that's OK" he said in his `public school-boys voice`……Bless him.


The farmer and his family returned to their house and we started to look around the cattle shed for our own home comforts.   No sooner had we settled down on our sleeping bags, we had a visit from the son and daughter with more coffee and waffles accompanied by a couple of their friends.   They broke into conversation with Lt. B-P and seemed to have the look of excitement all over their faces.   They soon left running back to the house screaming and shouting.

"What the fuck was all that about Boss"? asks Bob.

"Oh, the kids wanted to know if I would take them flying tomorrow when they finish school…little blighters" he said.

"And"?

"Well I will see what I can do I told them, lets wait for tomorrow, see how busy we are" he replied.

"Jesus!!!!!…. You will get `strung up` boss if this gets out you know" Ron said.

"But it won't get out will it; it's my helicopter while we are here".

He really didn't give a toss about anything!

The following day we were up early and got the cab ready for the days tasking. We then basically sat around drinking brews and chatting whilst the boss was away with the rest of the crew.

Because we were so far around the other side of the hill, as far as we were concerned, we were free of HQ prying eyes and basically not involved with the exercise i.e. patrols, sentry duties and the like....it was a doddle for us so we were making the most of it! The Norwegian kids ran down to see us as soon as they got home from school. We were kicking a ball around with them and their parents loved the fact that we were spending some time with them.

Not long after, the cab returned having completed the tasking for the day. Once it landed Lt. B-P waved one of our guys over and got him to get the kids in the back of the cab, the excitement on their faces was a picture! The father had ran down to us and jumped into the helicopter as well then Lt. B-P lifted into the hover and proceeded to give them a `ride of their lives` up and down this long field doing wing-over's from one end to the other.......they loved it!!

Later that evening we were getting a meal ready from our 24Hr ration packs when into the cattle building walked the farmer. Norwegian conversation finished with Lt. B-P, we had been invited up to the farm house to eat with the family....happy days we thought. Mother had cooked some sort of Reindeer stew with vegetables and we sat down and cleaned our plates, with a beer or two of course. After the meal we then sat and listened to Elvis Presley records with the family.............this is outrageous! Here we are, supposed to be involved in a NATO exercise in Norway costing `god knows how much` And Elvis is blasting out `Blue Suede Shoes` while we drink Norwegian lager in a farmer's house!!!

The next day came and went and so did the next and the next. Every other night we had our invite up to the farm house and hosted in luxury. While all this was happening to us, the rest of the Squadron guys were getting mucked in with the ongoing exercise (well done lads). We are now into our second week and Lt. B-P comes back from the farmer's house having spoken to him with good news for us.

"Chaps, Farmer and wife have said its ok for us to use their bath facilities should we wish to, they don't think its good that we keep using water from the stream to wash anymore what with the cattle and all" he pipes up.

"Brilliant, I'm up for some of that" I said and grabbed my dhobi kit (wash bag).

"Wait chaps, just hold on 1 second, I'm the Officer in charge and I did all the talking so I'm first in the bath, so sit yourselves down again, there's good chaps" Lt. B-P quipped.

He was a character was Lt B-P. You had to laugh at him, he was `typical` Public Schooling and had an accent that would fit into any High Society Occasion. Off he went for his bath.

On return he has more news to share with us.

"Chaps, when you go to bathe, farmer's wife has

requested that you take along any dirty clothing you wish to be washed and she will have it ready for us in the morning, ok?"

Hahahaha…      Branston-Pickle      you      are unfuckingbelievable!!!

Farmers wife **did indeed** do our washing and did it **again** on week 3 of the exercise!

Now, what I haven't mentioned yet is that during our 3 week period every day the cab flew back to HQ the crewman would pick up our 12 man, 24 hour ration packs.  3 weeks of food stacked up in a corner of the cattle building we were in!!  The kids had the sweets and chocolate from the boxes and we munched on the biscuits when we had a brew on the go…that was about it.  All the rest of the food had to be got rid of somehow before we packed up and flew to HQ for exercise de-briefing (not that we did much!).  Along with the ration packs we were given large tins of spuds and veg` also. We couldn't take it back with us as questions would be asked, nor could we dig holes and bury it (there was far too much of it).

"Got it" shouted Bob.

"Got it".

"What the fuck are you going on about Bob?"

"Let's give it to the farmer and his wife for being so good to us over the past 3 weeks".

We looked around at each other and thought, `well no-one else has come up with anything better, yeh lets do it`.

Lt. B-P and the crew were tasking for the final part of the exercise while we lugged the food boxes up to the farmers house. We were already packed up and ready to jump on the helicopter when it returned so all we had left to do was get rid of this lot!

Bob knocked on the door and let himself in followed by the rest of our Eagle Base guys carrying boxes. Into the kitchen we walked and stacked the boxes on the floor. It was obvious that farmer was not at home and kids were at school. Bob began to open up the boxes and take food out and place it on the work surface of the kitchen whilst explaining in his `Wolverhampton accent` what was in the packets and cans to the farmers wife.

Remember, wife does not speak English and we do not speak Norwegian.

"Bob, what the fuck are you doing? She hasn't got a clue what you are on about. Why don't we just leave the food and go wait for the cab" says Ron.

Bob then has the bright idea of matching whatever she has in her kitchen cupboards to whatever we have in the food boxes. Tins of Carrots, Powdered milk, Beans, Sugar, Rice, pointing to her tins then to ours, matching them up as he went. She was starting to get the drift until that is, when Bob picked up several cans of `Babies Heads`!!!! `Babies Heads` are more commonly known throughout the Forces as.......Steak and Kidney pies!!

Don't ask me where the saying comes from because I do not know, all I know is that they are called Babies Heads!

And delicious they are as well.

Bob searched the cupboards high and low but couldn't find anything that resembled what he was holding, both him and the wife looking confused as he was trying his best to explain what was in the cans.

"Bob, the cab is on its way back" came a shout from the doorway where we stood having a smoke.

"Come on mate we have to leg-it quickly" I shouted as the guys picked up bergans and kit and were making their way to the cab which had now landed but still with rotors spinning around.

"Lt. B-P is waving to us out of the helicopter cockpit window to come forward and I think he doesn't want to hang around mate".

True to my word, Bob took a can and placed it next to her baby's head. Her baby was lying in a sort of wicker cot which she had placed on the kitchen table. All the time Bob's shouting "Babies Heads, Babies Heads while pointing to her baby's head!!!

Hahahaha…you should have seen the look on her face as I pulled Bob out of the kitchen and picked up our gear whilst running towards the cab. We slung our bergans inside the helicopter and turned to wave goodbye to the farmer's wife.

She stood in her doorway, baby in one arm and a can in the other hand looking at both obviously very puzzled!!!

The cabin door was closed and we lifted and flew off. We landed a while later at the HQ and met up with the rest of the Eagle Bases.

"Hey up lads! How did you get on during the exercise"? We asked whist looking at this motley bunch that were as black as coal and stunk to high heaven!

"A fucking damn site worse than you lot by the looks of it"! Came a reply.

We were looking very fresh and clean considering we had been **living** in `the field` for 3 weeks!

"That bastard stream was freezing for washing in eh"? Said Nobby. "Really?

"Ours had running hot water" I replied!

All inquisitive enquiries over and done with, we boarded our helicopters and flew out to re-join the ship. The cabs were sorted out and put down below decks in the ships hanger, kit was cleaned and stowed away, we had 2 or 3 days to sail home....or so we thought!

"Captain speaking" came a voice over the ships tanoy announcement system.

"You will all be pleased to know that the exercise went very well indeed and we are now on our way home but we will be stopping off for 6 days in St Pauli, Hamburg as this will be the last trip for HMS Bulwark. I will speak to you more when we near Hamburg, that is all"

Oh yes indeed we like this we thought!!!

6 days in notorious Hamburg with the average age of us lads just 20 years old and what makes it even better is that for every day we have been away we have been paid an extra £12 a day.....1981 remember, that's roughly £360-£400 to blow in 6 days along with the money we have not spent whilst on exercise, so around about £1500 everyone has!

Whilst sailing up the river into St Pauli, Hamburg, we were shown videos of Hamburg and places to stay clear of. Needless to say we were making note of these places as they would be our first stop-off. Ship tied up along-side we made our way down the gangway and off into town pockets loaded up!!!

I'm not going to go into detail but you readers know what goes on in Hamburg so picture what you will in your heads for a minute or two......Ok done?

Having spent a couple of hours boozing and walking round the cultured streets, we decided to look in on the `Bier Keller` which sounded brilliant! Paid our entrance fee and shown to a table in the corner of this huge function hall we ordered our steins of ale with our lovely waitress. She returned not long after carrying about 10 of these large glasses brimming over with gods liquid, smashed them down on the table and proceeded to start chanting this German Bier Keller song....of course we all joined in with her!

The place was heaving and every table was packed with all nationalities but mainly German/Dutch and a lot of them dressed in their National dress of leather pants, white shirts with braces, white knee length socks and black shoes, standing up and slapping thighs as the Oompha Band on the stage blurted out those distinctive tunes!

It didn't take long before our table was awash with glasses of beer and we, along with the rest of the place were stood up on chairs clapping and dancing.

The place was buzzing!!

Stein  after stein after stein of ale, we really were getting into the swing of things, just as the band stopped playing and said it was.... `zee interval time`. Off the stage they went and everyone was either singing German songs in their groups, laughing, drinking, screaming, the place was so busy they didn't notice the `new drummer` get up onto the stage for a solo performance!

About 2 minutes previous to this, Jez says....

"Watch this, I'm off to play those drums"

and with that he surely was off.

Off to the stage.

"Go on Jez, go on son play those drums" we were all shouting as he sat behind the drum kit and picked up the sticks.

He bangs a drum and then looks to our corner smiling.

Bangs another drum a little harder and looks at us again....

All of a sudden he goes into a frenzy and starts banging the whole drum set like the character `Animal` who plays drums in the TV show, The Muppets!!!

Well, we are now rolling about in laughter as he is hitting this drum kit like it has done him some harm!! The rest of the place has now noticed that the guy playing drums is different from the one in the band and so has one of the door staff!!

Imagine from the front of the stage if you will, the tables were made of thick oak were placed together. Running from the stage in line down the whole of the Keller.

The Doorman (who is a monster of a man) is now running along side the tables towards the stage.

"Jez, Jez, lookout mate you have company coming your way" we are shouting whilst he still carries on banging his frenzied drum tune!!

As the doorman reaches the stage, Jez stands up off the drum kit stool, picks up a drum stick in each hand (the ones with the large white padded ball on the ends of them) and runs from the stage, jumps and lands on the first table!

The doorman who is now looking up at Jez tries to grab him but Jez is now off around the Bier Keller running and jumping from table to table to table with the doorman in hot pursuit running parallel to him! There's glasses' flying everywhere as Jez weaves his way through the beer filled tables. We are now rolling around `Laughing Kitbags`!!!

"Run Jez Run" we shouted (years before it was said in the movie Forest Gump).

"Run Jez mate, run, he's going to catch you".

All the time during the `cat & mouse chase`, Jez looked down at the doorman as he looked up at Jez whilst running along side him.....Jez slammed on the anchor and stopped running, he looked down at the doorman whilst still stood on the table and the doorman looked up at Jez........

BOPPITY-BOP-BOPPITY-BOP-BOPPITY-BOP!!!

went Jez with the drum sticks on the top of the doorman's bald shiny head!!. And off he went running and jumping again from table to table with the drum sticks in his hands leaving the doorman holding the top of his head!

Well, that was the final straw!

We all collapsed in hysterics as Jez was now being rugby tackled by the bald doorman with a `red shiny bald head` about another three tables on! He was taken to the main entrance and thrown out; we were all behind him laughing our fucking heads off!!!

Fantastic!!

Crying our eyes out with laughter we strolled in and out of bars throughout the rest of the night. I can't remember much more of that night or how we got back to the ship but when I woke up in the morning I had somehow managed to get myself stripped off and into my bunk. "What the fuck has happened" I thought as I felt my right fore-arm was bandaged up!

I got out of my bunk and stood there, still worse for wear from our epic evening and started to undo the bandage.

"Sshh, he's up".

"Sshh he's fucking awake" I heard being whispered around 2A mess on HMS Bulwark (the biggest mess in the fleet at the time sleeping around 100 guys).

WHAT-THE-FUCK-IS-THIS!!!!! I bellowed. WHAT-THE FUCKS-HAPPENED-YOU-SHITS!!!!!!!!

There (and still is today) is a tattoo of `Popeye`!
Not just any Popeye…oh no!
This Popeye has got a purple smoking pipe stuck up his nose!
A blue fucking bobble hat perched on his head!
Red fucking trousers!

And the name…`RICHARD M` tattooed underneath him!!!!!

"WHO-THE-FUCK-HAS-DONE-THIS"? I shouted at various guys still lying in their bunks, biting into there pillows screaming with fucking laughter!!

I checked my wallet…there wasn't much left out of 600 German marks!!

(About £150)!!!

To this day I know one or more of you tosses' reading this are 'Laughing Kitbags' as you know who set me up..............ah well, never mind, it was a good laugh anyway eh?

I still need to know though......

Who the hell is.... RICHARD M

Right then, here we go! From now on, the 'dits' get a lot more colourful shall we say. I **had** to write them like this to have the true context expressed throughout (I'm sure you will agree reader that it's the only way it can be done). So, for all of you with heart problems, high blood pressure or a very, very small tolerance to bad language?....I'm warning you now that this book is not suitable for you and that you must stop reading it, close it up and put it down! If, on the other hand you have the ability to not look at the world through 'rose coloured spectacles' and you can forget your inhibitions, let your mind roam and not 'judge a book by its cover', then I am sure you will have a laugh or 2 or 3 or 4 as you read on!........and remember, take it easy with the criticism eh I'm not an Author!

# CONTENTS

# 22 YEARS TO GO

Right, so this is how it all started.

Some of the pupils messed about and were not really interested in joining the Armed Forces.

Myself? I couldn't wait.

There I was, a sixteen-year-old sat at the front of the class at school hanging off every word these guys were saying. It was the turn of the Royal Navy Careers Team to come and marvel us with tales of the sea, ports to visit, further education to be had and of course a secure future. Having listened to them for about an hour, I could have walked out with them and signed the dotted line right there and then;

the last four months at school could not come quick enough.

My dad had served time in the RN as a stoker and like many other fathers, encouraged me to follow in his footsteps, I didn't need much encouragement.

Kenny Merritt, an ex-sailor himself lived next door and had served in the Fleet Air Arm and many a time I would invite myself into his house to listen to him crank out the stories while swigging from his never end supply of Newcastle Brown Ale which was in a crate down to the left of his arm chair. I remember laughing my head off along with his son Davey, at the way he tried to impress us with his ` women in every port` stories whilst knocking back another gulp from his Newc`y bottle.

He'd said enough for me though and before I knew it, I had left school and was waiting for my joining date of January 4th 1977 having completed my entrance exam.

The Fleet Air Arm as a Naval Air Mechanic was the way I had decided to go. I didn't even know the RN had aircraft but took a great interest in motor mechanics at school so thought, why not.

So, seeing my waiting time out, I was taken on by Binns, which was a large store in Sunderland, my home town, as a sort of `warehouse boy` come packer, "where the fuck is January?" I used to ask myself. Months went by and my medical was completed at Gunner House, Newcastle. Nick` my cousin came round to see if I wanted to go and mingle around the car warehouse / showroom which was near to my Gran`s. Fuck me, if we didn't get caught stealing a pair of those mirror type sunglasses, which were of all the rage at the time. Needless to say, me dad blew his lid, took me to the RN Careers Office in town and listened while I had to explain to this Fleet Chief Petty Officer what had happened. I was warned by them that should I drop myself in the shit whilst waiting for my joining date, I had to inform them as it would be worse for me should I get summonsed to court when I had just joined up. My joining date was put back a year…for the sake of a pair of poxy sunglasses.

The police gave me a caution and I thought afterwards,

shit!

If Id kept my gob shut no one would have been the wiser. Little did I know, it was about to stand me in good stead in years to come.

My joining documents, travel warrant and map had arrived.

Yes, map.

Don't forget here I am leaving Sunderland for a place called Plymouth; I could have needed my passport for all I knew. It wasn't long before I was stood on the platform at Newcastle Central, January 9th 1978. My old man had wanted to see me away and we stood grinning to each other whilst listening to stories of the deep that these four sailor's in uniform were gobbing off about. It didn't take me long to cotton on that they had joined HMS Raleigh just before Christmas and were now on there way back to carry on with there training, each one of them sounding like Long John fucking Silver.

The train came; I shook my old man's hand and left, Plymouth eh?

All I know is we travel south and turn right near the bottom of the country.

We arrived at Plymouth several hours and numerous stories later from the old and bold sat across from me.

Having been met at the ferry jetty by duty staff we were soon on our way to HMS Raleigh, the basic training Establishment.

It hadn't been long before I introduced myself to two Northern lads, Barry Trotter and Alan Watson. I noticed that there were a lot of cockneys around with us and thought it best to stick with my own breed as football grounds had been the only other place I had come across the southerners.

That evening we were given a very informal joining speech about where we were and what would be expected of us. I can't remember anyone taking a bite of notice as we all eyed each other up to see who was missing mummy already.

Next came the splitting into two groups.

Career or 3 yearly option i.e. 3, 6,9,12 and so on.

Out of a class of about thirty-five, there must have been only seven or eight ready for full career.

I was one of them.

No hesitation what-so-ever I signed the dotted line, took a copy from the instructor and sat down feeling very pleased with myself.

Kit was then later issued and we were shown to our mess deck.

Anson block had several messes and on entering ours we were given the statuary welcome from windows around us, I'm sure I heard the voices of our sea farers in uniform from on the train so I just let it ride over me.

Everyone was then left to mingle and meet each other. Some sat on their beds wondering if they had done the right thing. Others unpacked their worldly goods, while the rest met outside in the foyer for a smoke. Whilst working out one another dialects, we were interrupted by this monster of a fella who introduced himself as Simon, Simon Paley from the midlands somewhere.

A good six and a half feet tall and solidly built.

`Looks like I've been picked to be class leader` he said,

having been taken to one side and spoken to by the instructors.

No one questioned it.

He was softly spoken and had a vocabulary to that of which I last heard from my Literature teacher at school, I didn't understand her either. It became apparent that Simon had been a schoolteacher and had packed it in to look for something more fulfilling, he was aged about twenty-six, the average age of the class was around seventeen, I myself had just turned seventeen.

`Fifteen minutes fellas for lights out`, shouted someone up the stairway.

On walking over to the bed that I had chosen, I noticed that one of the cockney lads had parked his arse right next to me. Who would have known that we would be the last two along with an Irish lad out of the whole class to complete twenty-two years.

Day one came and went as quick as that.

I didn't know whether to wind up my arse or scratch my watch, we were all in it together though so everyone probably looked as bemused as each other.

I soon learnt over the first couple of days, that the next five or six weeks would be of a short sharp shock routine.

I was not mistaken.

Within the first week, the whole of our class was introduced to press-ups by the duty instructor in the courtyard, in our knicks` at daft o'clock in the morning and it just so happens, it was tossing it down with rain. The next time our mess got raided at around 01:00 we would be ready for them. Apparently, its part of the welcoming ritual to find yourselves was being whacked to fuck with pillows while you sleep and then your accommodation being turned upside down.

Being smacked around the head while I was in deep slumber was something I'd not been used to at home!

The visitors got quite a shock to say the least when someone dived for the lights; they had obviously not met our Simon. The few visitors left standing returned to their block soon after and needless to say, we never saw them again.

I returned to my bed for what was left of the night.

Every day started with the lights being turned on and a loud rendition of this bugle playing which reminded me of when the cavalry would charge against Indians in some John Wayne movie, again, this was not something my dad would do when waking me up for school.

The meals were adequate but meal times themselves were a pain in the arse as you would march to the galley, be ridiculed and mocked by the welcoming committee, eat your meal and then march back to the block. Classroom-drill-meal-Classroom-drill-meal day in day out. Time in the evening was spent sitting around the 'spit-kid' exchanging ideas on how to achieve the best shine whilst bulling' your boots.

The spit-kid looked like a hubcap off a dump truck. Strategically placed in the centre of the boot-polishing group, it would be full of fag ends and cotton-wool balls engorged in kiwi polish in no time. I reckoned the spit-kid had heard some cracking stories and introductions in it's time because we were all trying our hardest to outdo one another with the like. By now we have some real characters emerging. We've met Simon; we have Paddy Chestnut, knee high to a grasshopper and the first Irish accent I've ever heard outside of television. Barry Trotter, who looked like a spin off from Bob Haley and the Comets with his bufonted quiff, Alan Watson from Newcastle whose Geordie twang had everyone asking him to repeat himself. Barry (cor blimey me old china) Stuttle, could of walked straight off the Old Kent Road in his Pearly King suit. Dave Ringrow was the cockney fella next to me in the mess. A well built lad who turned out to know a few tricks with a football, he also raided his mother's kitchen of biscuits before he left home, finding himself most popular when a mug of tea was at hand.

Most nights were spent in the same company doing the boots or just trying to outdo each other with our stories.

I can not remember much of a social life during my time in training probably because most of the time in the evenings I would get my kit ready for the following days programme and then make sure I had some spare. You would see fellas twenty minutes before a lesson actually ironing kit, be it sport or drill instruction or kit inspections, which were as regular as clockwork. Once done though then it was off in evening rig (which was still uniform) to the NAFFI complex.

WRNS galore, it must have been paradise for those with a fetish of uniforms.

So there we were, thinking we were the `dogs bollocks` in uniform, smoking Pussers blue liner fags, four weeks under the belt and chatting away as though we had just returned from an epic trip…

sipping orange juice or lemonade.

Remember, that the majority of us were under eighteen and the Powers above did not look lightly on under aged drinking. Anyway, the ones who were old enough stuck out like sore thumbs the following day as they could...

`hoot with the owls but couldn't soar with the eagles`.

An expression I would hear time and time again throughout my career.

We were getting close to completing our basic training having had the obligatory dockyard visit, cunning ploy of the Mob` that was. Lads are still within the `premature voluntary release` stage, so a trip to the dockyard to relight the enthusiasm would probably do the trick.

Myself?

I was just enjoying the day out.

Well, six weeks were up and our passing out parade day was upon us. Everyone gleaming like new pins ready to impress the pants` off their loved ones and parents who had travelled down for the day.

Two others guys and I had another two weeks to go, we hadn't achieved the necessary grade in mathematics.

I was gutted to say the least as I watched my mates board the coach to take them onto their next stage which was HMS Daedalus near Portsmouth.

Here, we would be taught the basics of our chosen trade, Aircraft Engineering.

I couldn't believe it.

I knuckled down and achieved the grade in mathematics then caught up with the rest of the class at Daedalus. The routine there was a little more relaxed with regards to `bullshit`, not much though.

The course would last for sixteen weeks whereupon at the end of it I would have the choice of four Air Stations to go to and four different aircraft types to become conversant with. It didn't take long to realise that a bit of self-study in the evening was necessary as the tests and exams came thick and fast.

HMS Daedalus was an old Establishment that primarily catered for training Aircraft Engineers and was also the home of the Fleet Air Arm Field Gun Crew…

this I was very excited with.

I recall watching it on T.V. as a lad and couldn't believe it when I saw it at first hand.

The schooling started to decline slightly as most of my free time was spent down at the track side watching in disbelief as these fellas manhandled this gun and limber around, through and over walls and ramps.

Stand-easy, lunchtime and as soon as class would finish, I `d be at the track.

The thought of Aircraft, ships and Air stations all went out the window. This is what I wanted but being under training it was going to be impossible. Until that is when this fella, Eric Brotherton, asks me if I would like to take part in Brickwoods Field Gun. A very similar gun and limber to that of the Command Field Gun Crew but ran over a concrete surface against the clock with various tasks to be carried out, all with a team of eighteen.

Of course I jumped at the invitation.

My class instructor at the time was Petty Officer Ray Nicholson. A good bloke who's instructional technique was very relaxed. We would be half way through a system of an Aircraft, at probably a deep and meaningful point when he would whip out his fags, light one up and say` I remember when`…that would be it, we would be lectured on some foreign bars or nightlife for the next hour or so and it reminded me so much of when I used to listen to my old mans stories! I used this time to play catch up with my notes as the evenings were now being taken up with far more important things like Brickwoods.

Brickwoods training was going well until about a week before the competition where around fifteen Establishment teams would race at HMS Collingwood for various silver trophies, I sustained a bad injury that put me in the naval hospital Haslar for six weeks. The tendons in my right ankle were very badly sprained when my foot was unfortunately caught under one wheel of the gun. Needless to say the Engineering training school was not happy and neither was I.

I would again fall behind my class.

I suppose I should have requested permission before getting involved with Brickwoods but being under training, I knew the answer would have been no, so I made the most of six weeks in hospital.

Ray brought books in for me to study but the enthusiasm had gone.

I was released from Haslar earlier than I thought and on return to Daedalus found that I had to wait about two weeks for a new bunch coming through for me to join as Id fallen way back behind my class Whilst waiting, I met some fellas out of the class which was just in front of my original. Jez Daniels, Jock Husker and Billy Dainty.

I initially met them as they were playing some sort of football game in the recreational space of the mess with a `blow up sex aid doll`.

The next time I clocked eyes on the doll, it was hanging outside one of the block windows about twenty feet in the air with a rope noose around its neck dressed in WRNS clothing.

It just so happened that the Establishment morning Divisions were also taking place on the parade ground and everyone marched passed our block.

I think one Chief Wren nearly fainted, bless her.


The FAA Field Gun Crew had now left for Earls Court and the Royal Tournament; finally I could concentrate on completing this course and moving on.

I had now been with my new class for some time and the weeks were moving ahead. My original class was about to move to their chosen Air Stations and on the morning of their departure, I had a little score to settle. Barry Trotter had bought himself a Kawasaki 250 triple` motorbike and offered me a go one Sunday afternoon.

"Get yourself down the runway Ditchy, it's got to be quiet today". Thinking I was the legend motorcycle racer Barry Sheen, I hammered down the main runway on the Airfield and to my astonishment nearly collided with a group of people and their gliders.

Trotter was on the phone to the MoD police saying a nutter had taken his bike and was rip roaring around the camp, his idea of a joke I suppose when he seen the coppers close in on me.

So that morning of their departure at around 0500 I crept in on Trotter and carefully placed a match between each of his toes.

Not a normal sized match but the long domestic kitchen type ones, his feet looked a picture hanging over the edge of the bed all loaded up like Guy Fawkes Night.

I lit them and left.

As I am writing this I am laughing my fucking head

off because after 22 years I can still see him jumping out of bed and around the room like a scene out of a Tom and Jerry cartoon.

I waved them and their bus goodbye later that morning as I lit a fag up with one of these kitchen matches, Trotters face looking out of the bus window was a picture…I was never to see him again.

Anyway, you should by now have an idea of where I am going with this book. It is intended to give you an insight to some of the funnier times whilst serving my time within the R.N. Throughout the book, some names will have been changed not only to save face but to safe-guard against character deformation as many of the people involved are still serving, whether it be on the shop floor or as High Ranking Officers and no way are they taking me to court! So, Find a quiet spot, loose your inhibitions and try and picture yourself there whilst laughing with me. As they say… **"All Work and No Play Makes `Jack` a Dull Boy!!!"**

# ZX38

Royal Naval Air Station Yeovilton in Somerset was to be my preference draft to work on Wessex Mk5 Commando Helicopters after I finally completed my basic training.

On arriving there I met up with the rest of my original class to start on the next phase, which was the hands-on Engineering side. As time went by, new mates were made and the good times were about to begin.

As an impressionable young matelot, I along with my mates stood in disbelief as we witnessed our first ever Squadron comradeship!

The Commanding Officer of our squadron (he's remaining nameless) would stand on top of a box or small aircraft ladders whilst delivering his speech/brief to us all in the hanger.

He would then direct us all to group forward in front of him and at the top of his voice, shout…

"What are we here for"? to which we all had to reply…

"To kill Russians" whilst punching your right fist up into the air. Looking around at each other, I recall thinking….`fuck-me!!! Bring it on!

It was the night before our first set of Station Divisions and having recently finished basic training our uniforms were in tip-top condition, so a bunch of us decided to venture into town to check out which were the best watering holes. We came across a pub called The Albion (god rest its foundations, as it's pulled down now, but became our second home as will be discovered later on) and proceeded to get completely smashed! Why worry about tomorrow anyway, it was only about 4000 sailors standing there in uniform, some being inspected by an Admiral.

No way would a bunch of youngsters be put right in the front we thought…how wrong could we have been.

Jet` Weavers was a happy-go-lucky cockney who played guitar in a punk rock band when he was home on weekends and leave.

Why Jet?

Because his body hair was `Jet Black`.

We ended up back in our accommodation later that night task completed, as we were all worse for wear. No sooner than we striped off and got in our pits did Jet` burst through the door with a fully charged fire hose and proceeded to give us a fucking good soaking whilst laughing like a mad man. The hose was thrown down and off he ran to lock himself in his room. An hour or so passed and we managed to unlock his door, Jet` was out for the count so, armed with shaving foam and a razor proceeded to remove those big black eyebrows of his.

Take it from me; someone with no eyebrows looks like someone from the cult movie `The Hills Have Eyes`…Jet` was left to sleep.

We woke to the screams of……..

"You bastards!!!!"

"That'll be Jet" someone said.

Having got `shit-showered n shaved` we stood in our uniforms grinning from ear to ear as we listened to Jet` pleading with the Squadron Regulator to be stood-down from that morning Divisions.

"Unlucky Jet you're in the shit! On divisions you go my lad" said the Regulator with a sadistic smile on his face.

Hiding my tears of laughter I coaxed Jet` into using this grease on his face.

ZX38, black and thick, it's what was used on various parts of the aircraft.

From about 10 feet away it really did look like Jet's own eyebrows. "FALL IN"….. came the command from the Gunnery Officer as thousands of sailors and WRNS moved into their respective platoons. Shuffling for position, Jet` ended up in the front rank of our platoon and our platoon just happened to be in the front row of the whole fucking set-up!

Shit! we're going to be inspected first we thought.

Not only are we suffering from hangovers but we also now have to concentrate on not pissing ourselves in front of a full Admiral and his high ranking officers whilst in uniform on our first major divisions.

I say concentrate on not pissing ourselves because Jets temporary eyebrows are now beginning to melt in the mid morning sun!

Everyone in our platoon including the Seniors has now got those stupid uncontrollable `school type` giggles, very difficult not to get noticed when you are

15

stood to attention, tears starting to well up in your eyes and between 40-50 officers are stood about 30 feet away facing you ready to commence with the historical event.

Every now and again, Jet would swiftly bring up his right arm and rub left & right across his eyes to remove what he thought was sweat running from beneath his cap. The sun got higher and the volunteer band played on. Not only was the thought of Jets face sending us into hysterics but the band decided to do their usual of cocking up several notes here and there which made them sound like a `Les Dawson sketch on the piano`, this we found very amusing.

So, the scene is set.

The band is doing their bit, we are in stitches and the sun is beating down on Jets face that, what with all the wiping now looks like someone out of the 60's TV programme `The Black & White Minstrel Show`. God knows what a sight it must have been for the on looking Officers and by now a few of us have drawn blood because of biting our lips as not to collapse in a blithering shitty heap.

The duty vicar conducts the sermon and at this point, caps are removed and heads bowed while he prays for us and blesses us. It gives us a bit of breathing space while Jet is frantically trying to wipe this muck off his face................

"AMEN"

"On Caps" came the order from the Gunnery Officer.

Jet now looked like a pint of Guinness!

What with his black face and his white sailors cap. I was in fucking fit's, just as I am now whilst writing this, as I can remember it as though it was yesterday.

The band resumed its jaunty tunes whilst the inspecting Officers proceeded to march out to their respective platoons. The Admiral started his inspection of a platoon that was a couple to the right of us along with the rest of his entourage. This gave Jet even more time to sort out his face, every ten seconds or so his arm would shoot up and he'd wipe his face with his uniform sleeve which didn't matter because the uniform was dark anyway.

"Quick Jet, quick he's nearly here" the lads were whispering. "STAND STILL" shouted the Gunnery Officer...too late Jet, he's here. We couldn't believe our ears when Jet replied to the Admiral that he had a skin complaint when asked what was wrong with him and that the cream he was using had an adverse effect on bright sunny days. His face was more of a light chocolate brown by now but his hands were as `black as coal`.

You lucky bastard we thought as the Admiral moved on throughout the platoon, and then came that old saying `Bullshit Baffles Brains`, not to the `Fleet Master at Arms` it doesn't though.

He, I suppose is the `dad of the pad` when it comes to anything dealing with discipline! Noticing the state of Jets hands, he leant forward and whispered in his ear to see him on completion of divisions. The whole ceremony was finished with the march past the Admiral and his fellow officers who would `take the salute`. The Admirals face was a picture if I remember rightly as he glared at `Jet` when we were given the order...`Eyes

Right` as we marched past the dais. Later that day and we wandered off back to our accommodation to get changed, Jet had gone to see `the man`. Some time later Jet returned to the accommodation his face back to its natural colour. His punishment would be to report to the Fleet Master at Arms office every morning for a week making sure the tea was ready for him and his team by the time they walked in the office. He would then be subjected to a barrage of questioning from the Regulators to what had happened that night on the Establishment, if anything at all. Anything for them to get their teeth into, quiet daunting when you have six or seven `Rat-catchers` pounding you with questions at the same time. Needless to say, Jet made the tea and said fuck all.

# FLASHDANCE

So, here we are having jumped ahead a few years and I find myself off to Lebanon with my buddies on the Squadron. The Squadron at the time had some right characters on there and it was definitely a case of `work hard, play hard, play harder`!

The ship, RFA Reliant, was already out sailing around Cyprus with our Helicopters on it just waiting for the signal to go in and extract British citizens and troops out from Lebanon when the `shit hits the fan`! I flew out to Cyprus with the rest of the crew that was to take over from the lads who had been out there for quite some time. Dave Bolton flew out with me and I was looking forward to having a good time with him.

After landing at the RAF base in Cyprus we got a small boat out to where the ship was anchored. Boarding the ship, kit stowed, and bed made, it was time we had a look around to familiarise ourselves with our home for the next how-ever months!

"Coming ashore tonight then fellas?" asks Lou.

"And just how are we supposed to get ashore then?" Dave questioned back.

"Mate, the ship is running Liberty boats when we are anchored off Cyprus and the last one don't come back till

00:30, so you can have a wail of a time ashore" replied Lou.

"That'll do for me Ditchy boy" said Dave and with that he was off to get changed into civvies and await the first boat ashore.....I was right behind him.

As Lou said. The ship was running a Liberty boat service at times when it sailed back to anchor just off Cyprus from its operating area just off the Lebanese coast. The coming Sunday, it would pull up its anchor and sail back to the `box` as we knew it to await for the extractions signal, whereupon our cabs would fly in to an open area and fly out as many British citizens and troops as fast as they could before the American war ship, USS New Jersey, opened up and flattened the place!

"Don't forget to `peg-out` before you climb down the ladder and remember, the last boat back is 00:30, Don't miss it"! Ordered the Duty Officer.

"Look at the bright lights, look at the bright lights" Dave said as we made our way to the jetty at Limasol.

All of us were looking forward to what Cyprus had on offer, especially the ones who had not been there before.

"This way then lads" said Lou.

He had been here for a month or so and knew where the best bars were and with that we were off the boat and strutting through town with a spring in our step, hands being rubbed together in excitement! We spent the night visiting various haunts and getting the feel of the place when we came across a dancing bar........Dancing bar meaning that it had girls dancing on a make shift stage in front of an audience.

"Haven't got enough time for this one" said Lou,

"The last boat back to the ship leaves in about 20 minutes".

Lou was off down to the jetty with others to catch the last `taxi` back to the ship.

"Just a couple of minutes" said Dave as he ordered two bottles of local brew.

Jesus! They are lovely aren't they? "Got to come back here again" he said all excitedly.

"Yeh, alright mate but I suppose we better make tracks down to the jetty for the boat" I replied.

On turning the corner which led down a cobbled pathway to the jetty we saw our lift back to the ship chugging on its way!!!

"SHIT!"

"Erm, yes mate, I think we have just dropped in it" I said as we watched the last boat steaming along with Lou and Co. waving to us no doubt laughing like kids! We sat down, lit a cigarette and thought about our options......................... Needless to say, we didn't have many!

"All we can do mate is wait for the fishermen to turn up at daft o` clock in the morning and scrounge a lift off one of them" I suggested. "Suppose so mate, might as well go back to the dancing bar eh?" He said.

A couple of minutes later and we had a bevy of girls dancing seductively in front of our eyes............ Gorgeous!

Time was now about 04:00 and we decided to stagger down to the jetty where we would put our well learned Cypriot language course to the test! Neither of us could speak a word of it and the fishermen were no better at the English language!

After a short while though we got a fisherman to understand what we were requesting and having parted with god-knows how many Cypriot pounds, we were on our way back to our floating home which by the way was due to set sail for our `box` just of the Lebanon coastline at 06:00. With about 1 ½ hours to spare we had made it and climbing the rope ladder back on board we were both very surprised to see the Duty Officer had waited up all night for us and welcomed us both back with early morning tea & toast....NOT!!

"Not a good start at all gentlemen eh?" he quipped.

"I'll peg you back in and expect to see you both 08:00 sharp in the Regulating office" he said with his back towards us.

Bed-time we thought and quietly.

08:00 came and we both stood there in the Regulating office, side by side, and took the biggest bollocking ever....full blast and roughly about 3 to 4 inches away from our faces.

The Ships captain was not impressed at all (even though he was of the Royal Fleet Auxiliary, and looked upon as civilian); he gave one- hell- of- a -bollocking! We kept out of his way from then on.

Weeks went by where the ship would sail from its anchor point to the `box` on Sunday morning, sail round and round the `box` for 2 weeks waiting for the go-ahead and if the signal was not sent by late Friday of the second week we would sail back to Cyprus waters and anchor off.

We had been out there a couple of months during which time came close to having a bit of a confrontation with these so called `gun-boats`. Fuck knows where they were from but they decided to come and have a go at us and whilst they were heading our way we loaded up as many GPMG (general purpose machine guns) as possible and waited for them to get within range. The ships captain meanwhile had the ships engines full steam ahead and was trying to out run these things...

What the hell was he thinking of ? Bring it on we thought.

Our fun soon diminished as an American military plane flew over the top of them making them turn and get the hell out of there immediately! "Oh well, shit happens" said Harry,

"lets get back to the sun-bathing".

You see, if we weren't working on the cabs, you were sun-bathing. When the cabs were flying, you were sun-bathing. If you were not doing anything else, you were sun-bathing! Not much more to do than sun-bathe, stuck in the middle of the Mediterranean Sea going round and round and fucking round!

At last!

Time to go in and do what we came here to do.

The ship had received the signal to put into operation the extraction of British citizens (mainly government staff) and British troops from Lebanon. We got our cabs airborne and off they went not knowing what crazy bastards were on the ground! The local gangs, military, groups, hoods, call them what you will, were fighting for street corners, that's how it was. Myself, Lou, Harry and a couple of others got onboard a Chinook helicopter that had landed on our ship and before we knew it, was given a short brief on the American M16 assault rifle while we sat on the deck of the helicopter as it hammered low level over the Lebanese bay. The seats had been taken out of the helicopter to accommodate as many people as possible and to get them out of there as quickly as possible as the USS New Jersey was going to open up its Big Guns on the place at 16:00…every thing had to be done by then, if not earlier!

The helicopters needed a crew on the ground to under sling the vehicles to them when they came in to hover.

We were that crew.

On running out of the Chinook when it landed, it became apparent that this was not going to be such a `walk in the park` as we thought it would be.

As I've said, there was gun fire virtually on every corner of a street and buildings around us. Gun fire not directed at us but an ongoing feud that has gone on for years between the local fractions living there.

Don't go questioning me about the politics of it all as I haven't got a fucking clue, all I know is that there's dozens of our Army lads (The Queens Lancers) and their vehicles wanting a lift out of this god-forsaken shithole!

Women, men and children queued orderly and were directed to helicopters as they landed, quickly as possible scurrying on board. Once full, up and away they flew, back to our ship where if they were not already on one, they would be transferred to a Chinook helicopter which would then fly them to the RAF base in Cyprus.

Helicopter after helicopter came in, loaded up and left, this went on for hours!

The number of British civilians started to dwindle and so the Army lads were next. We got them back on board the ship just as quick and then proceeded to under sling their vehicles back to the ship where they would be lined up and nylon lashings attached to them to stop them rolling around should the ship hit bad weather.

During all the mayhem that was going on we couldn't believe what we saw next...........

We found out that some bloke has a light aircraft and is charging an extortionate amount of money to fly the husband of whoever back to a landing strip in Lebanon from Cyprus for him then to retrieve his bonds, jewellery, and whatever else these government people hide away in banks and then for him to run down this street with all manner of shit going off around him and then to jump back on to our helicopters!!!

Believe me...You could not make this up!!

I think these dickheads could read our minds so there was no need to say anything to them!!

15:30 and we are out of there, knackered!!  16:00 as advertised, the USS New Jersey showed us all why at that precise moment it was, `The biggest Kid in the playground`

It went on for hours, unrelenting shelling of pre-planned targets...........We, along with the guys from the Queens Lancers sat on the ships deck in the early evening sun, drinking beer out of the `Watneys Party Cans`.  Bet there's a few of you who remember those eh?

Well the Lancers whilst queuing on the roadside saw that the locals were helping themselves to a supermarket and other stores around so, as not to leave any trip hazards lying around, the lads picked up the said `party cans` (which held about 7 pints I think) and packed them inside their Ferret armoured vehicles!

Nice one lads!

Unbeknown to them though, Robbie Burns and a

few others of the workshops staff had raided the vehicles and had the more precious stuff (i.e. whisky) away whilst they were been lashed down on the ship.

So, now the shenanigans are over and done with, what now? We ask ourselves.

Well its back to Cyprus for a start and anchor off as usual then await further orders.

"I've heard through the grapevine, that we are to have some time ashore me old shipmates" pipes Harry and we have beds waiting for us at the RAF base, how fucking good is that" he beamed.

It was true; we did have beds waiting for us courtesy of our `Crab` (RAF) buddies. And so, we flew onto their base until we knew what was to happen to us next.

"Lets not waste any time then mateys, lets go have a look at what luxuries our friends have" shouts Harry and with that, we were off to their bar.

Their bar was just that......a bar!

Standard duke box in the corner, a few potted plants, a sort of 2x1 inch slatted wooden frame work that segregated the lads from the Corporals and 3 Cypriot guys selling the drinks over the bar.

The bar.......

"Yeh, great idea this one Harry, I've seen more life in a fucking morgue!" I said.

"Well why don't we play a game or two then?" and with that he threw a metal ashtray from the table we were sat at up into the ceiling fans whirring around above us.

"Jesus mate! Did you see that fly?" screamed Minnie.

The ashtray flew like an Olympic discus when it made contact with the fan blades and now everyone wanted a go.

Only now it was a game of.............

`Let's see who can hit the barman` as they ran the length of the bar from left to right dodging the incoming metal discus.

Well it kept us amused for a while and as the wine flowed....

YES, Wine.

It was only 11p a pint!! Tasted like 11p worth as well!!


"What about this then" as Minnie threw toilet rolls from out of the gents' loo into the said fans and set them alight, watching fixated as the loo rolls unwound whilst spiralling with flames! "Good eh?" Beamed Minnie..............Little bit crazy was Minnie but he was a good lad and a good chef too.

He was a Royal Marine who had been given as an attachment to the Squadron and he made a mean stew when we were in field conditions .... Yeh, good lad was Minnie.

"Christ! That wine has gone through me like a dose of salts! I'm off to the bog!" said Stan.

Little did Stan know that Minnie had all the toilet rolls down by the side of his chair and that Stan would have to adapt and overcome when it came to sorting himself out!

"What the hell are you doing?" shouted this bloke stood in the loo door way.

"I'm the Duty Orderly Sergeant and I'm telling you to get your fat arse out of that sink now!"

Stan looked up in amazement and was indeed now sat with his fat arse in a sink of warm water, lapping it up with his hand whilst holding onto the sink with his other! (Because he couldn't find any loo roll.......good thinking Stan).

"Oh really...Well I'm the Duty Disorderly Sailor" answered Stan

"and if you don't mind, I'm trying to CLEAN-MY-ARSE!!"

Needless to say, we were asked to leave the bar........... no problem, we were on our way anyway.

We cleaned the place up, left the bar staff a huge tip for the fun they had given us and left for town as we had a dancing bar to visit!

So, picture the scene.

About a dozen of us having had a good slurp of wine at ridiculous prices, sat in front of this dancing stage which is of a half moon shape. We are sat at eye level looking at the dancing girls and enjoying the performance.

They were doing a raunchy routine with backing music from the early eighties movie, `Flashdance`.

Some of you may remember the dancer in the movie who, during a dance routine she runs towards a wall in the dance studio at the same time doing a split jump in the air and then with agility, speed and ability, does a run up the wall and kicks her legs up and over to produce a backward somersault off the wall, landing back on her feet and starts to dance again!....

Fantastic!......Well.....

The dancing girls have finished for a break and our friend Minnie is now stood on the stage with his arms stretched out wide shouting....FLASHDANCE.... FLASHDANCE "Play the music for me.... FLASHDANCE".

We are sat there in awe of Minnie as all the fella wants to do is dance. So, there we all are sat next to a load of locals in this bar waiting to see if they play the music for Minnie who is now stood on the edge of the stage warming up. Oh and by the way, the back wall of the stage has a full mural painting on it and for all we know…..it's a wall.

Boom, boom, boom…….the music started up and true to his word, Minnie started to dance, all by himself on a stage in a bar in Cyprus. Brilliant.

The locals too were enjoying it as they were clapping to the music as loud as us and egging Minnie on!

Then it happened!!!!

The chorus started and then……..
"FLASHDANCE…FLASHDANCE"
shouted Minnie as he started to run at full pelt towards the back wall of the stage. Before anyone could shout anything, Minnie had started to run up the wall with a view of doing a backward somersault, just like the movie!!!!…..

I kid you not!!………….
At a height of about 4 feet…

CRACK!!

Minnie's legs went straight through the wall… (The timber partitioning wall that was).

All that anyone could see of Minnie was the top half of his body from his waist upwards flailing around in a hole in the middle of this mural painting!!

Priceless!

We got up and retrieved Minnie from the `hole in the wall`……….. The place was in uproar and it goes without saying that a few of our lads were lying on the floor `Laughing Kitbags`!!

We decided to make our way back to the base as it was now early hours in the morning and word on the street was that we may be flying tomorrow. On returning back the base, Lou thought we should finish the night off with a little party, a sort of `pat on the back for us party` for all the good work we had carried out. So, whilst walking back to where we were sleeping, Lou shouts out…..

"This place will do"

and with that he opens the door to somebody's room. These rooms were like the type you would see at a Butlins Holiday camp years ago. Lights came on and…….

"Let's be having you then me lads, we have decided to use your gaff for a party of which we are allowing you to join in with us or you can take your beds outside as it's a lovely evening?"

The two guys sat bolt upright in their beds looking at each other as though to say…..

"What the fuck is going on here?"

We lifted the beds (with the guys in them) outside onto a grassed area and whilst we were sifting through what music they had, we had Minnie go to the bar and purchase a couple of crates! Music was playing and the sound of beer bottles being opened filled the evening sky, we were all in jovial mood and Harry was keeping our hosts happy by sitting on one of their beds out on the grassed area telling them dits` of who we were and the like………..their faces were a picture……they must have thought "are we dreaming this or what?"

"I do not fucking believe it"…..gasped Minnie as he rooted through the guys c.d. collection.

"They only have a FLASHDANCE c.d. haven't they!!!?"

You could have heard a pin drop as everyone looked towards Minnie with mouths wide open.

"No way Minnie, not again I said….you will cause fucking mayhem on this camp if we go through that again", even though everyone wanted to see him try the backward somersault trick again!

Party over………….we again cleared up, lifted our hosts in their beds back into their room, thanked them, turned the lights off, closed the door and left.

I wonder if they got back to sleep that night?

Well, tomorrow is Sunday and we have an invite to the water-ski bar down by the waters edge courtesy of our RAF chappies! True to their word, we turned up on mass at the water ski-bar at mid day and our hosts were there in force. Unbeknown to us, they have in their company, the RAF champion water-skier. Lots of beer and story swapping later our Squadron is challenged to a water ski competition. `Old water wings` himself goes first and does things on water that the majority of us would find hard to do on land. We all watch from the patio area around the bar which looks out over the harbour. One after another, again and again our lads try to perfect and sometimes try and dazzle the hosts with water ski-ing tricks. It was like watching Bambi on ice!! Needless to say, the beers were on us and the RAF had the last laugh but then we heard……

brrrp-brrrpbrrp-brRRRPPPPPP,

getting louder and louder, coming down the roadway onto the boat slipway and OFF, OFF

into the sea went one of our pilots (who will remain nameless) OFF into the sea on the Camp Commanders motorcycle!!!!!! Now we have the last laugh..........Oh yes...............we stood, laughing kitbags!!!

# GOOD TIMES ALL THE TIME BACK THEN

Saturday early mornings were usually spent watching `Tiswaz` whilst nursing a hangover. As soon as we woke up we would hop over the road to 61 mess (845 Sqdn) in our sleeping bags and congregate around the colour TV. Guys would be just rising out of bed from the aftermath of the previous evening, the usual smells lingering in the air!! We would sit around in the television room which was situated on the end of the mess. The mess would sleep about 20 guys all with their bed spaces cordoned off with extra lockers like a kids `den`...Jim Hunter probably had the best `den` that I saw. In the corner of the mess, 4 lockers he had, (2 at the side of his bed & 2 at the bottom of his bed) with string tied between them and a blanket draped over the string for his doorway to his bit of sanctuary. His little portable black & white TV and an ashtray full to the gunnels.

These messes were of the post war Army type, long and narrow with wooden flooring throughout and the toilets/showers stuck on the end of it, unlike the single en-suite cabins young matelots have these days!!

No sooner had we re-heated Friday evenings left over Chinese take-away on an upturned iron (no microwave ovens), we would be planning the rest of our day. As the morning rolled on `dits` would be swapped as who did what with whom that previous night…..every Friday was Market Day! The pubs in town would stay open from 12 mid-day until 12 midnight…how we looked forward to Market Days. Mind you though you were expected to help out with the publicans also, by that I mean, you would be expected to empty ashtrays, return glasses to the bar and in one pub `The Kings Arms` it would be expected of you to pick up the bucket & mop and mop through. The bar staff in the `Mermaid` could have you with the vacuum in hand, hovering the beer stained carpet. All this to get the place ready for the evening session. Each pub would stop pouring ale for about 15-20 minutes to clean up after the afternoon session at around 5 o'clock but if you timed it correctly, you could leave `The Albion` lets say and by the time you walked to `The Mermaid`, `The Greyhound`, `The Hole in the Wall`, `The Globe`, `3 Choughs`, `Wine Vaults`, `Butchers Arms`, `The Pall`, or `Kings Arms`, the clearing up would have been done and so no quaffing time missed! The late evening would be spent in Electric Studio, Carnabys or Pandora's nightclubs. (My god, what's happened to the place, here we are in 2010 and there is 3 or 4 pubs with `Chicago Rock pub` pretending it's a night-club, that's about it).

Sunday lunchtime would be spent over in the Heron Club all rates bar where the lunchtime entertainment would usually be that of some Country & Western singer strumming his guitar. On most occasions he would be politely asked to leave during his session whilst his equipment was being dumped out of the windows! Usual suspects would then set up the bar microphone and we would then have a free-for-all sing along!

Now that was better.

One particular Sunday afternoon I remember, was when a team of the lads challenged a team of females to a charity rugby game out at the camp. The females team was made up of cleaners and bar staff from Carnabys night club in town and had named themselves `The Carnaby Crunches`. After the game, a sociable drink or two was had in the rugby club which was just around the corner from the Heron Club…and that's all I'm saying about that particular day.

Not even I could write down what went on!!! Ha-ha-ha.

Sunday evenings would see Navy buses turn up at the main gate with girls from town and the surrounding villages.

Tuesday evenings would see Navy buses turn up at the main gate with girls from town and the surrounding villages.

Thursday evenings would see Navy buses turn up at the main gate with girls from town and the surrounding villages.

For these evenings were `Bop` Nights…….with our own resident D.J. (Robbie big-thumbs) all going on in the `Heron Club` with the unfortunate `Duty Watch Shore Patrol` stood outside peering through the bar windows.

The Regulating staff along with the Executive Dept

thought it would be to their advantage to have Navy buses ferry a load of females onto the camp rather than have the matelots going in town to the pubs.....ha-ha-ha, who thought that one up? There was more 'goings-on' around that camp on 'Bop Nights' than there was in Soho ha-ha-ha...nice one!

The visiting girls even had there own I.D. cards and had to sign in when entering the camp!!!

And so, Mondays & Wednesdays would be recovery days and boy! Did we need those days?.....No actually that's not true.

Mondays was also Market Day in town and Wednesday afternoon was taken up with either a football or rugby game of which most of us played for the camp and so afterwards a few ales were the norm'and so, a full week was virtually every week!

For those of us working up at the Squadrons when it was a 'bop night', when all the work had been completed it was expected of you to go to the 'Men's Bar' which was situated around the corner of the 'bop' with your 'Watch Chief'. Still in working rig and stinking of aircraft fuel & grease, a few sociable beers would be had. Some of the lads though thought it a good idea at 22:30 to travel from our camp in Yeovil to 'Bristol beer Keller' in working rig, have a good night out, drive back and still turn-to the following morning at 0700 to do whatever was required of them.

It was a case of 'If you are 'hooting with the owls' late at night then you have to be able to 'soar with the eagles' early in the morn'.

Anyway, back to Saturday morning eh?

Lunchtime would be upon us and the Navy would put on a duty civilian driver to take us into town in the duty bus. First port of call was usually `The Globe`. Guys would do different routes so as not to overcrowd the bars. The majority would meet up mid afternoon in the famous `Albion` pub.

Now, that was a pub!!

One particular Saturday we had decided that we would though go to the `3 Choughs` for a change of start venue. As the day went along guys would be playing one another at pool.

"Aye, fucking beat ya again Fossy, aye ya nee good Fossy" said Peds to Stuart with his Big Scottish grin plastered all over his red face!

"Let's see how good you are when you've had a good skin-full eh?" replied Stuart and at that got the next round of ale in.

Time rolled on and off we went to various other pubs visiting one of our favourites, `The Hole in the Wall`.

"Cider all round please Liz" I said and Liz the landlady would fill the glasses whilst eyeing us up and down to see if we had had enough already.

Liz was very eccentric and old fashioned she also didn't stand for any nonsense so we behaved ourselves when in her pub. A few pints later and then "Come on the Stuart, I'll give ya another chance ta try an beat ma?" said Peds, offering him to another game of pool.

"Not interested Peds, I'm on the cider" replied Stu.

It must have been an hour or two before we somehow ended up back in the `3 Choughs` pub. I cant remember how it came about but Stuart had been challenged by

Peds that he `bets Stuart £10 that he cannot run out of the pub, up the pathway and back in the other door before he pots all the balls on the table, leaving just the black ball` oh, and Stuarts got to do it naked!!

Saturday afternoon, middle of town, about 3 o'clock!!

Peds puts the money in the pool table slot, Stuart starts stripping off, Peds sets the balls up on the table, Stuarts only got his shoes and shirt off, Peds starts potting the balls, Stuarts down to his Knicks and socks, Peds has now got 4 or 5 balls to pot, Stuart is naked and now exiting the pub, Peds drops his pool cue and bolts for the door which Stuart is running to and wedges it closed with a chair, Stuart bangs the door and realising its closed about turns and is now running back to the other door, Peds inside the pub runs to the other door and has now got his fat arse up against the door stopping Stuart getting back in the pub!! Ha-ha.

We all stood with our pints watching out the windows as shopping folk were commenting on Stuart, Laughing Kitbags!! We then all stood pissing ourselves with laughter when Stuart came into the bar and was looking for his clothes.....

`Jesus, look` shouted Ali as he pointed to Stuarts clothes going up in flames on the pub open fire! To this day I can't remember who put them on the fire but I think it must have been Peds as he ran passed them to block the doorway. Stuart got the fire tongs and started to whip his clothes out of the fire and then picked them up and took them to the toilet to soak them to stop the burning.

Peds went back to playing pool as we waited for the

`burnt-cinder kid` to return. Stuart walked back into the bar smouldering ha-ha-ha!

Peds shouted "Here Stuart, watch this black ball go down", as he was trying a difficult shot. Whilst Peds bent over the table eyeing up his shot, Stuart walked over and picked up a pool cue.

"No, let's watch you go down" he said and.... `SMASH`!!

Peds was down alright as Stuart broke the fat end of the pool cue over Peds` head! Good old Peds ha-ha.

If the weather was nice, we usually went to the beach...Yes, Yeovil has a beach!

Well, it's what we called it.

It was the grassed area in front of the town main church and everyone knew it as `The Beach`. Yeovil is in fact about 30 mile from the nearest beach. One day whilst sat on the beach having a drink or two, the sunny day became overcast and rain descended upon us very quickly.

"Hurry up lads; we will get in there till it stops eh"? Shouted Ali whilst we picked up our flagons of cider and ran towards a yellow rubbish skip parked at the side of the church. Being of relatively young age still and not so much loose muscle (fat), we managed to clamber through the square cut out in the side of the skip only to land on newspapers and magazines inside. A tarpaulin on the roof kept us dry. Happy days, here we are dry, comfortable and with enough cider to keep us going for a while. Having been in there about 30 minutes with the rain lashing down, a couple of lads had dozed off whilst lying on the newspaper stack.

"Oh I say, what's going on in here then"? Questioned a little old lady to Billy as she threw a plastic bag of magazines through the skip cut out slot and Billy took them off her.

"What you up to then"?

"Well madam its like this, we are doing our bit for the community by being in this skip, as we are sorting out these newspapers and magazines into bundles to make it easier for the collection people and them guys sleeping over in the corner have been in here on night shift"

"Oh I say, you are good boys aren't you, well done boys, keep up the good work".

Billy rolled back into the newspapers laughing kitbags as she poked her head through the skip slot and started waving at us all.

Another particular Saturday that springs to mind was the time we were all getting ready, (shit-shower-shave). Myself and (the kid...he`s still serving) were having a deep and meaningful conversation whilst having a `number 2` (him in the next trap, obviously).

"Right, that's me then" he says which he immediately followed by shouting "Look-out... soft Grenade!!"

and at that, I looked upwards to see the said `soft grenade` coming over the top of my trap!!!

My god...enough to give you a heart attack!!

Thankfully I had a newspaper with me to cover over my head as the `soft grenade` impacted on me!! `I will have to remember that one` I thought to myself as the day ahead is long. Having jumped under the shower and cleaned myself more than usual due to the `soft grenade`, I made my way back to my mess-deck which was next door to (the kid) having popped my head round his door to thank him for his toilet gift and that I would be re-paying him. He was there, sat on his bed showing off his new stereo system to a couple of the lads, turning the music up full, and windows rattling. Chuffed to bits he was with his new buy. Ian 'Taff' Davies was Leading Hand of his mess. In-charge of the guys and their welfare and has gone up to (the kid) and notified him that,

"If that shit gets turned up anymore, its going out the window!!"…he was blaring out the sounds. 'Mmmmm I thought to myself, I will remember this for later on' and went next door to my mess to get ready for the days adventures! Off into town we popped courtesy of the duty Navy driver and his bus ha-ha-ha.

Sometime had passed and all I remember next was the fact that we were back at camp and we have had our fill of ale! It's daft o'clock in the morning and I've remembered that I owe (the kid) one. Creeping into his mess next door, the smell when I opened the door was horrendous!! But trying to be as quiet as possible, I made my way around to his bed space and on opening his locker doors I picked up the remote control of his Stereo system.

'Click-click-click-click went the volume dial as I pointed this remote at it from inside his locker, doors about ½ inch open.

Click-click-click…'little bit more I thought' and then…………..

BOOM-BOOM-BOOM-BOOM-BOOM!!

'Fantastic mate, fantastic'

I thought as (the kid) leaped from his drunken sleeping stupor, screaming and trying to hug these massive speakers whilst being stark-bollocked-naked (in pitch darkness). The rest of the mess occupants jumped with shock as well from there drunken sleeps. Boots and all manner of things are being thrown towards (the kid's) bed space…man he took one-hell-of a battering.

BOOM-BOOM-BOOM went his drum and bass music as he was trying to squeeze the life out of these speakers!! Taff came stomping up to his bed and pulled the plug out of the wall. "What the fuck do you think you're doing?

You fucking idiot, get to bed and keep that shit off, you dickhead"!

Taff screams at him, all the time (the kid) trying to explain to him that he doesn't know what's happened and that he is all confused and that he is sorry` and

"sorry guys wont happen again, promise" ha-ha-ha-ha

Oh fucking really?

Well we shall see about that, I thought.

Sunday morning and (the kid) is still getting grief from the other guys in the mess as I walk in. He's trying to explain that there must be something wrong with his new purchase but the guys are having none of it.

"What was all that fucking noise last night?" I said.

"That dickhead and his music box" replied Taff (not impressed at all).

"Come on, the club is open soon, lets get going" I said to the guys and off we went for our usual Sunday lunchtime session.

Sunday afternoons were usually spent quaffing cider from the `Navarac Club` having smuggled it onto the camp in a boot of a car. `Navarac` is caravan spelt backwards and this was a living site full of caravans for married couples whilst they were waiting for married accommodation to become available. This is where we got our cider!

Sat outside the mess with the cider concealed in dustbins (deep trouble if found with alcohol on the camp) on a sunny Sunday afternoon with a handful of resident wrens with us…mmmmm!

And so, Sunday night `bop` was upon us and as usual it was packed, last weekend session before work tomorrow morning 0700 sharp!

`The Quartermaster` at the time was a good mate of mine, Bren Wilde. He was seen as the `Officer of the Watch's` right hand man. He would pipe the `still and carry on` during the raising & lowering of the flag through his `Bosuns call whistle` and make general piped announcements throughout the camp over the announcements system as directed by the O.O.W. amongst a lot of other duties.

A `piped announcement` throughout the camp usually went something like… "Do you hear there" A.E.M (aircraft engineering mechanic) SMITH, contact the Guardroom, A.E.M SMITH. This would bellow out around the camp and even over in the Officer's accommodation. This position was seen as an important position to be in and one that required a lot of tact and diplomacy as a lot of the time you could be dealing with general public enquiries as well.

On the said evening, Bren was on watch in the Guardroom whilst the rest of us were enjoying the Sunday night `bop`. The navy buses as per usual were ferrying in the local talent and everyone was having a good time. There was a girl I remember who, sorry to say it…absolutely stunk to high heaven!!!

Her nick-name was `Armpits`!!! Phew!!

She was always in desperate need of soap and deodorant…phew!!

Anyway, as the evening went on, announcements were being made for this and that by Bren when all of a sudden we heard,

"Do you hear there? Quartermaster speaking, A.R.M. Pitts contact the Guardroom, A.R.M. Pitts"…he then repeated this announcement about 30 seconds later… Jesus!!!!!

She went berserk!!

She ran over to the Guardroom with a pint glass in her hand and was threatening to glass Bren with it who was by now hiding behind the Officer of the Watch…her language was even to blue for me to repeat in this book!! Ha-ha-ha-ha!

It was hilarious though.

Bren was removed from being Quartermaster the following day by the Captains 1st Lieutenant!!


Right, back to the dit…Now where was I?

Oh yes, we were having our night in the `bop` topping up from a pretty good weekend. The Bop has finished and lads and lasses are making there way back to there accommodation. Duty shore patrol are trying to keep order and there's a massive queue outside Max`s burger wagon serving up the usual overpriced, overcooked cheese burgers and chips or you could go to the guy who was parked up outside the main gate in his wagon. He was outside the main gate because he was always `pissed-drunk` when he turned up and was not allowed onto the camp but could park on the road outside as this was a public road.

Guys would help themselves when the drunken burger chef left his wagon to have a pee!! I made my way back to the mess and pre-loaded (the kids) music box, for he was to have a surprise coming to him later!

It must have been `daft o clock` in the morning again when I decided to pay a visit to (the kid) and his marvellous music box! Once again on entering his mess, the stench of stale beer and farts hit me and I found it hard not to start coughing! Into his locker again and up, up went the dial as I flicked the remote control.

"Sssssssssh".......BOOM-BOOM-BOOM-BOOM!!

Up out of bed whilst screaming and hugging the speakers leaped (the kid).

BOOM-BOOM-BOOM-BOOM.

That was it, lights came on and god knows how many boots were thrown at him, smashing off the locker, whacking into the wall, knocking all manor of stuff all over the place. His bed space was a shit-tip!! And all he could do was say,

"sorry fellas" in a sort of `what the fuck is going on` voice.

I was stood in his locker nearly pissing myself with laughter!!

It took a while for everyone to settle down again and when it was all peaceful, I left.

I really wanted so much though to take the remote control with me and crank it up again from outside a window!! For the following day and for about a week after, no-one in (the kids) mess would speak to him. He felt really shit and was pleading with guys to forgive him as he didn't want to be singled out ha-ha-ha-ha…

I watched for a while then decided to come clean to (the kid) and the guys!!

There's a time when I was employed on the buffers party whilst waiting for my front line draft coming up and we had a few run-ins with the P.T. staff. It all started when Pete & Bob of the Physical Training Dept: had stolen the buffers section bike and managed to put it on top of the section roof. Chief of the section was John Anderson and basically gave us a free reign to inflict a bit of damage on the P.T. Dept. Having retrieved Chiefs bike from the rooftop, we boarded our flat-bed wagon and headed for the egg farm just outside the camp.

Eggs purchased, we got back onto the flat-bed wagon and made for the Establishments stables.

"Horse manure please" I asked one of the stable girls.

"How much you wanting?" she asks me.

"Oh, about a locker full I suppose" and at that started to shovel horse-shit onto the flat-bed wagon of ours.

Sat on the back of the wagon, hands loaded with eggs, we drove back through the main gate at very slow speed hoping to bump into Pete and Bob. Round and around the camp we drove, stopping to look round every corner.

"Got to be round here somewhere?" says George.

"Here Dinger, drive us around to the P.T store" he asks and at that we are driving slowly through the main gate again (even the O.O.W. was laughing at us as he knew what was going on).

On arriving at the P.T.store we jumped from the wagon and took up position around the store building. Peering through windows to see if the coast was clear, I opened the door and checked the place out.

"No fucker is home fellas, lets get that horse-shit in here" I shouted.

We proceeded to unload the said horse-shit...... straight into Pete's duty locker where he kept all his P.T.whites, his training kit and his spare P.T. white plimsolls!!! A few 6 inch nails just for good measure hammered in around the doors and draws and we were off! Chief received a phone call back in the buffers store not much later.

"Truce" was all that was said. Ha-ha-ha!! Yes, it was good times all the time back then.

# ABERYSTWYTH
# TELEPHONE
# EXCHANGE

The Gulf conflict was in full swing and we (845 and
848 Naval Air Commando Sqdns) were stuck in the
desert with our sister sqdn 846 playing` postmen pat`
on board a carrier taking it easy out at sea somewhere.
During the conflict we had the most difficult task of
sifting through loads of letters from females back here,
most of them wanting to meet up when we returned
home. Our mail distribution guy at the time was Pete
Smith, a Chief Petty Officer on 845 and also my landlord
back in England and not forgetting to mention, a bloody
good mate. Unbeknown to me and everyone else, Pete
used to open the mail, sort out the `definitely yes ones`
from the may be`s and then pass the rest out to the lads
(obviously keeping the decent ones himself).

As time went by he informed me that he had been
writing to this lass from Aberystwyth and showed me one
of his letters he had received from her.

Talk about horny… Pete couldn't wait to get home
and I could understand why.

This lass was ready to do everything to his `war torn`

body on his return and all he had to do was turn up at her place. Pete though, in his sexual stupor had sent a photo of himself but as letters were sent and received, he never got one of her…. (Mmmm, sounding dodgy already).

The conflict was coming to its final stages for us and we had come out of it unscathed, we are now waiting to go home. Whilst waiting on the tarmac of Kuwait International Airport wondering 'who the fuck' was going to get us out of this shit hole, Pete came up to me with a very inviting proposition. You see, the Arabs were quick enough to get us there, 1$^{st}$ class only in a Jumbo and all, giving out Free Kuwait Badges, free meals, drinks, flags, the fucking lot but could they be arsed to get us home?

Could they fuck!

And so we had to wait around with nothing to do apart from plan how we were going to celebrate on our return. Pete's last letter from Aberystwyth had said that her and 12 of her telephone exchange mates (all female) were hiring the whole top floor suit of this posh hotel and Pete along with whoever wanted to go would be welcome.

Sounded good.

As I was lodging with him back home, I thought I might as well go along and enjoy myself. It turns out that everyone else he had asked has decided to go straight on leave when they get home. So, Pete and I are off to this hotel suit, all paid for with 12 females…

Happy Days!

On arriving home Pete phoned Aberystwyth straight away, talking about this and that, who's going to do what and where, what the other girls names are and so-on.

Friday came and off we go (Aberystwyth knew that only two of us were going, as we found out later she didn't tell the other girls).

"The pub opposite the train station is where we will meet" she said, no problem.

Within a couple of hours we were pulling up in the car park of the train station having driven slowly passed the pub. Looking in his re-view mirror, Pete went `as white as a sheet`.

"What's up mate?" I asked.

"Look behind us slowly" came his reply.

"Fuck me! Its Astrix the Gaul," I said.

Aberystwyth was running across the road with a mate towards us, in one hand the photo of Pete (idiot) and in the other, a red rose! Dressed in trousers of blue and white stripes (the kind Astrix wore) and white Mini-Mouse high-heeled shoes and weighing in at around 14 or 15 big stones. "NO, NO, NO, FUCK NO!!" screamed Pete whilst banging his forehead on the steering wheel;

I was nearly pissing myself with laughter.

"Fuck it, if we just pull away they will never know and I will ring her up and say I had to visit my family" said Pete in an absolute petrified way.

I was still laughing kitbags!

"Look Pete we're here now, we might as well get out the car and meet them and who knows? Her mates at the hotel may be fucking stunners" I said whilst biting the inside of my mouth to stop me from dropping to my knees in a blithering heap when we got out the car.

"We will have a drink and if it doesn't sound good we are doing a runner O.K." he said.

I had to agree but I <u>definitely</u> wanted to stay because

I knew how this `wild child of Wales` had built up her hopes and was ready for a weekend of non-stop passion with war torn Pete. **I must stop for a moment because I cannot write due to the tears running down my cheeks... (It's one of those; YOU HAD TO BE THERE MOMENTS to believe it).**

There we both are, leaning on the boot of his car amazed as everyone else in the area, as this girl is bounding towards us `clip-clop clip-clop` in her white high heels waving this rose shouting at the top of her Welsh voice, **PEEETE, PEEETE.** Our eyes pissing out tears, trying hard to control the schoolboy smirk we have splattered across our faces.

**"Oh my god, I really didn't think you were going to turn up, anyway, I'm (Aberystwyth)"** I've forgot her name **"and this is so-and-so, you are obviously Peeete and you must be George"** she said with the biggest smile on her face which I must say resembled a dot to dot book with all the zits!

She had obviously spent time on her hair but forgotten such things as shampoo and a brush. The make-up was plastered on; finger nails non-existent and was proud to show off every curve and line of her body with the figure hugging Astrix the Gaul outfit! I held out my hand to acknowledge them, my eyes red raw with muffled laughter whilst Pete just sat there on the boot in shock and disbelief.

"Yeh...... yeh I'm Pete" he said,

**"EEE look", "doesn't he look like Michael Cain the actorrr,"** she said to her mate.

Pete does resemble him slightly but it's the way she came out with it that made me dive for the public toilets on the train station to relive myself in more ways than one. I got in there and absolutely `balled` my head off. Onlookers must have thought I was mad or something as I threw cold water from a tap over my face and constantly telling myself to `pull my fucking self together`.

Pete was right behind me.

We eventually came out to be greeted once again by Astrix and her mate.

**"Fancy a drink first does you boys?"** she drawled in her Welsh accent. By the look on Pete's face I would say he needed more than **a** drink. Anyway, no sooner had we got inside the pub opposite the train station Pete rushed to the bar and ordered two triple vodka & coke. **"Hitting the hard stuff straight away eh lads?"**

If only she knew, we thought, If only she knew!

We sat down and listened intensively to the plans that the girls had in store for us that weekend.

The vodka and coke kept flowing.

Because Pete and I had been the only ones to turn up, it was decided by Aberystwyth that we both stayed at her parent's house, as there was plenty of room and that it wasn't worth going to the hotel. So, half pissed, we followed her to her house. On meeting her parents it was decided that Pete would sleep in her room and she would share her sisters' room for the weekend. I was more than happy with the couch and a couple of blankets.

"What about the hotel" said Pete;

"Fuck it Pete we're here now lets make the most of it" I said and we sorted ourselves out to go out with the girls of the telephone exchange that evening.

"Want to come and meet the rest of the girls do you? They're dying to see you" she said?

Bloody right we do.

So arriving at the exchange having perked up a little, our faces went like smiling Cheshire cats as we looked up at the windows to a greeting of frenzied girls waiting to meet up with someone they had been reading about in the Gulf conflict not so long ago. Every man for himself we thought as we were ushered into their coffee room where upon we were inundated with women.

"This is so and so and this is so and so" went Aberystwyth, introducing us to all.

When they realised that Pete and I had been the only ones to turn up it became quite interesting listening to the conversations around the room and a few times we felt like lambs to the slaughter but we were not complaining too much! All of a sudden, in walked the envy of the exchange. Petit, blonde, very good looking with a stunning figure and everything else that went with it.

"Is SHE coming out tonight?" asked Pete

"Oh no no, we haven't asked her, you wouldn't like her, she's really stuck up she is" said Aberystwyth.

Neither of us got to speak to her as we were whisked from telephone operator to operator. They were as protective of their find like lionesses and it became obvious that the `blonde queen` was out numbered! Pete's face dropped once more as we were ushered out of the room and out of the building by Aberystwyth and her fellow lionesses, I just had a stupid smirk on my face constantly because I, like Pete, knew he was to be Aberystwyth's main course and she was not going to give him up to anyone.

My mind went back to the letters in the Gulf and thought `serves you right Smith, I hope she roots you all fucking night`!

So the time came when we had to hit the bright lights. Pete and I with a dozen girls from the exchange minus the blonde, damn!

From bar to bar we drank like true sailors and continued to impress our hosts as we could still manage to dance like John Travolta even while being pissed as a newt. Not known to them, that this is how we always danced it was just that the booze made our legs and hips a little more pliable than they were.

We ended up in a pub where her mother and father were, (who may I say were different altogether). By now we were relaxed for the simple fact that we had polished off a few Vodka/cokes and 6 or 7 pints but Pete was and had been for some time now in the trap of Astrix.

She had been linking his arm all night as though to say `look at my new play thing`…Mother was so pleased that Astrix was happy and was probably making plans for the future of her daughter. Hahahahaha !

I will never forget the look in Pete's eyes, as though to say

"will you please fucking help me", but I just carried on drinking thinking to myself `bollocks` Pete, I'm having a laugh on you! And he knew it.

The time came when everyone started to call for taxis and saying their goodnights.

**"Enjoy yourselves lads"** came a voice from the taxi queue; it was the blonde from the exchange.

She had been out with friends to all the usual bars

that the girls frequent hoping to bump into us. No wonder we had been taken to some shite places, so they could keep us away from the blonde bombshell!

**"Off you go then driver"** said Astrix and we was soon on our way back, Pete worrying about the sexual onslaught that she had in mind for him. I was with one of her friends who I had quite a good night with but on returning home, she was fit for one thing only.

Vomit!!!

And so with mother and father in bed, Astrix sharing her sisters' bed and me on the couch with some lass stinking of puke, I lay there giggling uncontrollably like some school kid, thinking about Pete and whether or not he would get a visit very shortly from his sex goddess.

Mother opened the curtains in the lounge and woke me in the morning. God knows what she must have thought as the room was in need of some very powerful air freshener, of which I did not have. So up I jumped and made my way upstairs to the bathroom only to see Pete packing his weekend bag in the bedroom. "What gives oh great stud of the valleys" I whispered.

"That's it, we are fucking off as soon as we've had breakfast" he quietly replied.

"She only came in at daft o` fucking clock and tried it on didn't she" said Pete. To which I immediately fell on the bed and laughed my head off.

"You didn't did you"? I said as my eyes welled up with tears.

"No I fucking didn't ranted Pete". She got in bed and started to manhandle me like a piece of fucking play dough, but I though, just keep snoring Pete and tossing and turning and she will fuck-off".

"Well, did she?"

"Yeh, she gave up after a while and said something about tonight's another night, so that's why we are leaving as soon as we have had breakfast" said Pete.

**"Breakfast is ready boys"** came the call from mother.

Sat there was father (nursing a hangover); sister was looking disgusted at Astrix and Astrix herself looking frustrated and full of sexual desire for Pete, who in turn kept his head down while tucking into his breakfast. I tried with great difficulty not to choke on mine as I had constant visions of Pete being mauled in bed just a few hours previously. **"Looking forward to your Sunday lunch then boys"** said mother?

**"I've heard it's a lovely place and so reasonable too".**

I looked at Pete, he looked at me eyes wide open and then Astrix said that she and the girls had booked several tables at a local pub/restaurant for lunch. Since she found out that only Pete and I were turning up, she had cancelled them and kept a table for four. Me, Pete, Astrix and the girl who had been vomiting virtually all night.

**"Yeh, 12:30 the table is booked for and then I thought we would go for a stroll through the local woodland"** she said.

Pete's face was a picture;

I very nearly blurted out a mouthful of breakfast at him across the table as the blood drained from his face. Pete had gone into shock or was that fright!.

Once again I had to excuse myself to go to the toilet were upon I cried into a towel as so to muffle my laughter,

56

whilst having a piss. Had I not done that, I would have seriously pissed in my pants!

Walking towards her friends' car, I made sure that I sat in the front next to her while Pete had to squeeze in the back with Astrix. If he could, he would have throttled me at least a dozen times that weekend but I was not letting down my defences and always made out that we were having a brilliant time and that we were thinking of staying longer. As it was, we said originally that we would stay until Monday but Pete had other ideas!

"I'm just off to the loo, wont be long" said Pete.

"I've done it," he said while we were at the bar.

"Done what?" I asked.

"I've phoned Rocky back home" he was lodging in Pete's house and he gave him the phone number of Astrix's mother and briefed him on what he wanted him to do.

"You crafty fucker Smith, what are you up to?" I asked.

"You'll see," he said whilst beaming a confident smile.

We returned back to Astrix's house full of Sunday lunch and depleted of Gulf hero stories of which I made Pete out to be the ultimate warrior and of the heroics that he performed. Needless to say, that Astrix was full of admiration for Pete and that one thing and one thing only was in her eyes...

LOVE!

I had stitched him up good and proper for hoarding all the letters in the Gulf (I also gave Astrix his mobile telephone number) just incase she wanted to keep in touch with her sweetheart!  Mother was sat on the sofa crying, father was still nursing his hangover in his comfortable chair.  **"What on earth is wrong mother?"** said Astrix as we entered the lounge.

**"Oh Peete, Peete"** cried mother as she wiped away more tears.  **"We've had a phone call earlier from a Lieutenant Rock and he wants to speak to you immediately, they have been trying to track you both down all weekend and I think you may be in trouble"**

Pete's face was a picture.

He looked at me as though to say….Fuck you!  I could not believe what I was hearing.

"Well I had better ring him and see what it's all about" he said.

Pete left the door to the hallway ajar, as he knew everyone would be listening.

"NO…….. Please say that you are having me on," said Pete, a slight pause and then…

"Well if that's what's going to happen, we shall return straight away Sir".

I thought, you crafty wanker!

"We have got to go back now," said Pete as mother, Asrtix, her mate and sister started to bawl their eyes out, father was still feeling very sorry for himself in his chair.

"Fuck em Pete" I said.

"Look, we have been missed all weekend, what's another night going to matter? We might as well stay here and travel back first thing, anyway the girls have organized a party round one of their mates and looks like we will be staying there tonight," I said convincingly.

**"Yes, please say you'll stay Peete, please"** begged Astrix.

"I'm sorry (Pete stood with his hand up in the air) but we must return and as a responsible Senior Rating in the Royal Navy, I must take charge and make a decision and I say we return back to our unit, anyway it sounds as though we are going back out there".

'Fuck me Pete; pile it on a bit more, why don't you' I thought.

The girls are crying their eyes out now and Pete has won the day! We went upstairs to pack our weekend bags and Pete was in raptures around the bedroom, I was once again biting a pillow to muffle my hysterical laughter.

"Come on" he said, "We've had a laugh now let's fuck off home".

As we got into Pete's car the whole family came out into the street with white handkerchiefs, waving. Even the neighbors' came out to see us off. As Pete pulled away, he wound his window down and shouted.........

"I'll write".

I nearly had heart failure.

"Come on Pete, lets get out of here" my cheeks and jowls aching with continuous laughter! The first thing Pete done when we got home was to buy an answering machine.

Needless to say, he didn't return many calls.

# ROYAL MARINES
# V THE SNOWMEN

Every year the Squadron would send 2 or 3 helicopters up to Norway so the Aircrew and Maintainers and Royal Marines could carry out winter survival exercisers and flying operations.

I had been there many, many times before and always enjoyed the place, hard work and hard play!

One particular time I remember well was when we had our cabs up in the air and we were sat around drinking coffee and playing cards. The Norwegian Air force police had already put a stop to our `drip tray sliding` as they found it to be dangerous!

Drip trays are made out of light Alloy and are used to collect fluid leaks or spillages and are placed under the helicopters when they are in the hanger. They also make excellent sledges when up in Norway! We would sit in one and hold onto a length of rope which would be tied to the back of a land rover. The land rover would speed off down the taxi track along side the runway and when you `lost your bottle` you simply let go of the rope and off you went on your drip tray.............great fun!

Anyway, like I said, the Norwegian police did not

find this amusing and stopped our fun! So, sat round a table in a smoke filled room watching 3 or 4 guy's playing cards, or drinking coffee, is all we had while the pilots were out doing their thing.

"Let's build snowmen?" I said to the fellas sat with me. They looked at me and after a pause...........

"Yeh, ok, lets see who can build the biggest?" as they proceeded to get their coats on. Snow in Norway is not a problem in winter, enough for all the kids in the world to have a good time in.......it just so happens that at this moment, we are the biggest kids! Snowmen building got on the way and things were going well. One lad went into the hanger to collect stuff to dress his snowman with, stuff like old rags, nuts and bolts for eyes etc`. One guy had ripped the head off a mop and used it for long hair on his and it looked a treat!

"Fellas, there's a land rover coming towards us with headlights flashing and I think I know what he has in mind" said Pete as he stood watching the vehicle pick up speed as it closed in on us.

"Fuck!!.... Everyman for himself" he shouted as we all dived in different directions as the land rover plowed at top speed through our snowmen!

`BOOF, BOOF, BOOF,

one after another the vehicle smashed through our pride and joy snowmen, we had been at it for about 2 hours now with the occasional snowball fight in between and we were pissed off at whoever it was in the vehicle! The vehicle turned and came towards us as we were dusting ourselves down from where we had dived to one side into the snow embankments.

"Hey, hey lads..............that's put your lights out

eh....hahaha" smirked this guy sat in the passenger seat whilst shouting out the window as they drove passed.

"Tosses' come on fellas, we'll build em again but this time we will build them over here" I said.

So on we went, back to rolling the base, collecting the stuff for the outfit, rolling the snow ball bigger and bigger.................Christ what am I doing?.... all you readers know how to make snowmen!!!!

Anyway, about an hour later and the helicopters have been back for fuel, gone again and are due back to base in about ½ hour. We had finished our snowmen, 3 in total, all stood together in one straight line and looking magnificent. Off to the hanger to get the bags of Arctic covers out ready for when the cabs land and shut down.

"Look fellas, I think we have visitors again" I said, pointing to a rogue land rover coming towards us with lights flashing...........".Let's stand back and watch them demolish these shall we?"

SSSSSSSSSSMASH!!!

The land rover stopped instantly when it ploughed into the 1st snowman! We walked over to the occupants who were two Royal Marines now sat looking all dazed and confused with steam pissing out of the front of the vehicle!

"Hey, hey lads..............that's put YOUR fucking lights out eh..........hahaha" I said

And we walked away to the landing area to wait for our cabs returning whilst laughing kitbags at these two dickheads that had just smashed into a concrete bollard!!!!!! Obviously covered by the snowman!

The last mini bus back from the local town was 01:00 and if you missed that then it was a case of a Norwegian taxi or you were walking back!! Everything about Norway is expensive and the taxi was not always favoured. So, nine times out of ten if you missed the last transport it was a case of head tucked down, hands in deep pockets, point yourself in the right direction and start walking!! The road back to camp was straight and not very long, about 30 minutes walk, so you couldn't go far wrong but it felt like an eternity when the wind was whistling around your ears! And you are trudging in deep snow!

At the time, a guy from the Army had been attached to us while we were there for the sole purpose of driving the big snow bucket. The snow bucket was basically a big JCB tractor with a huge bucket scoop on the front of it and was used to clear massive amounts of snow away from the operating area for our helicopters…..we named it Barry…..Barry the Bucket!

Anyway, this guy had wandered from his mates who he was out with that evening and found that he had missed the last bus back so, head tucked down, hands in deep pockets, pointing himself in the right direction he started to walk back to camp………..oh and guess what?………it is not the night you want to be walking back, it is absolutely perishing!!! Half way down the road which is dimly lit by the snow blowing against him as he walked; he sees a vehicle parked up on the side with its engine ticking over. On closer inspection and the nearer he got to the vehicle he could make out through his squinted eyes that it was a B.V. `Fantastic` he thinks to himself. I'll get the lads to give me a lift the rest of the way back to camp.

This B.V. is a vehicle which is used a lot in Norway as it is a tracked vehicle and ploughs through snow with no problem. It can be used for transporting people or stores as its drivers section is separate of the back section and is basically two vehicles coupled together and the engine powers wheels like any other vehicle but this has tracks around its wheels. It can also be used as a rescue vehicle but the majority of the time it is used with communications boxes fixed in the back compartment which doesn't leave much room for anything else apart from maybe two guys as operators.

So, matey-boy decides he will approach the driver and ask him to give him a lift back to camp which is about a ¼ of a mile further down the road. When he looked in the drivers' window he saw no-one! `But the engines ticking over he thinks`……..`maybe they are out nearby walking around patrolling` he thinks to himself.

`I can drive Barry the bucket so I suppose I can drive one of these` he thinks and at that in his drunken stupor, he gets into the B.V.

Into gear and off he goes down the road thinking…. `I will park it up just inside the main gate and head off to bed…the driver is bound to find it when he walks back to report it stolen`.

He gets to the main gate and acknowledges the Norwegian gate staff with a flick of his lights, they lift the barrier up and he drives through into the camp without stopping whilst waving and smiling at them.

`Fuck it, he thinks………..I'm going to have me some fun before I get my head down` and remembered the snow embankments he had created earlier that day with Barry the bucket! Off he goes down to where the hanger is situated. On seeing the snow banks he goes up the first one, over the top of it and down the other side. These snow banks are about 12 feet high! BRRRB,BRRRB,BRRRB..........up and down, round and round, turning the back-end on a sixpence, BRRRB,BRRRB.........the diesel engine working flat out.......up again, back down again, sling the back end round, BRRB,BRRB........... He was having a wail of a time!!

This went on for 5 or 10 minutes and then he decided to park it up back near to the main gate of the camp. He got out and left the engine ticking over just as how he found it.

As he was walking away from the vehicle with a large smile on his face, all he heard was......................

"WHAT-THE-FUCK-IS-GOING-ON?!!"
As he started to run over the football field back to his block he turned to see the rear door open and two guys fall out into a `shitty heap` on the ground!!

It later turns out that the two guys in the B.V. had been the two Royal Marines who earlier that day had smashed into our snowmen and wrecking a land rover in the process!

They had been given patrolling duty for the week as their punishment and that evening was their first evening......hahaha...they were laid down in the back of the BV zipped up in their Arctic sleeping bags keeping warm!

I think they had a few more duties after that when they had to try and explain all the dents in the rear compartment from where it had been smacked around!! I would have paid good money to have had a video camera in the back of that vehicle. Hahahahaha!

# WRONG PLACE AT WRONG TIME

"Haway man it wasn't mee man" said Stuart to the bouncers as he was led on his merry way down the stairs of Carnaby`s Nightclub and out into the street. What with his broad Geordie accent, fuelled with copious amounts of ale, he did not speak softly.

A Newcastle lad through and through had also served time in the R.N. Well known throughout town as a character that was game for a laugh and boy have we had some laughs!

I gave it about 10 to 15 minutes before I decided to follow him out. Apparently, he had been caught up in some commotion whilst in the club and bouncers being bouncers, grabbed whoever they could and ejected them, questioning them days was not an option.

"Am ower ere man" came the dulcet tones from my little Geordie friend. He was hanging onto a lamp-post with one arm and his other was draped around a lass whom I had never seen before.

"What's happening then Stu?" hoping to be introduced to his female friend.

"Well mate, am knackered and am ganin yam wi ower lass" he spurted.

"Where are you staying then?" she asks me.

"Erm…I'm staying at Stuarts this weekend" as a matter of fact.

At that, a taxi came whistling around the corner and up to us.

"See you later mate", as I opened the taxi door and pulled her in with me. Stu just held onto the lamp-post with that stupid drunken grin plastered all over his face, the kind of which I had seen many a time before (when something was not quite right).

"Lyde Road please drives" and off we went.

The taxi dropped us off and she said that she might see me around town sometime and that she was off home.

"Why don't you come in for a drink?" I asked.

She didn't need much persuading as she took hold of my hand and walked me up the path to Stu's front door.


On opening the door, I heard the most hilarious laughter I had ever heard and there on the sofa drinking from a flagon of farm cider absolutely pissing themselves was Stuart and another fella called Dusty Miller.

To this day, I still don't know how he made it home before me. Anyway, I went into the kitchen to get some drinks and thought that I would try my luck.

"You can go upstairs if you want to, 2nd on the right; I'll be up in a minute".

Not a word spoken, off she went and as she got onto the stairs, looked into the kitchen with that `Don't be long big-boy look`.

I thought, you've only gone and done it haven't you. The drunks in the lounge were nearly being sick with laughter as I looked in on them. "Don't go fucking it up now lads" I said and at that Stuart replied

**"you already have man"** with tears rolling down his face.

I've known Stu a long time and thought `yeh you'll soon be asleep, pissed again.

Mind you, so was I, but I was determined to succeed with my newly found.

As I opened the door to the bedroom, I realized that only one bedside light was on and walking into the room saw that my newly found was already in bed, gear all over the floor with the quilt pulled up to her chin. I thought I was King Dick as I walked around the bed and put the drinks on the bedside table. She lay there just looking up at me, as I undressed not saying a word and all the time I was thinking....

`Wahay` here we go!!!!!!!!!!!!

Trying to focus on the matter at hand while Pinky and fucking Perky were still in fits down stairs!

As I got into bed, she turned and said,

"Would you mind turning the light out?"

No problem I thought and leaned over to switch off the light. At that she grabbed my arse and gave it a squeeze. I was thinking, Am I the lucky one or what and proceeded to embrace her. She was as horny as hell and by her sounds was loving every minute of it as I kissed her neck and started to caress her `top-shelf`, which may I say were without doubt the best I had ever felt.

Full, lovely shaped and with the biggest nipples I have ever seen!

I could have done with a key from the side of a Corned Beef tin to unravel them; they must have been all of 1 inch erect!

It wasn't long before I was sucking on them like a hungry baby, which was obviously sending her doo-lally!

I too was getting very excited myself, I think because here I was in bed with some lass whose name I even didn't know, never met before, with great tits and she's all over me. All the time thinking, Go- on- my- son!

We had been working each other up for some time and I thought, right, let's go for the kill. My hand followed the lines of her body down to her treasure chest................. OH FUCK, oh fuck!!

What-on-earth-is-going-on!!

Here I am in darkness, in bed, with SOMETHINGS cock in my hand, sucking on IT`S tits!!!!!

I was out of that bed with my back up against the window in lightening speed. Having turned the light on, I was as sober as when we had gone out at 7p.m. that evening, but shaking through shock and horror. Standing there with fuck-all on, my brain was running overtime trying to put words into my mouth (which was now definitely better than IT`S nipples!).

"What the fuck is going on here?" I shouted.

IT now looking up at me, quilt pulled back up to IT`S chin.

Now, what you have to do is try and imagine the voice of Kenneth Williams (the actor out of the Carry On films, him who talks through his nostrils) because this person was now sounding like him.

**"MMMmm, you don't want to know anymore do you? Don't you want to suck my titties anymore, eh?"** it said.

I sat on the opposite side of the bed;

my back towards it and while quickly getting my clothes on said,

"Just get your gear and fuck-off". I was shaking like a leaf!

My head was spinning and I'm thinking to myself over and over…

Why me?

Why me?

In fucking Yeovil, Somerset as well, not Bangkok or Amsterdam or the Philippines!

why the fuck me?

**"So, you don't want to get to know me more then eh?"** as it propped it's self up on one elbow.

Glancing over my shoulder, I thought, fuck me what a great angle……………

SMASH!! and into its nose went the first right hand quickly followed by another to the left ear.

I'm now in a frenzy and it is about to receive some serious blows. THUD!! in went another as I connected with its chin.

My hands instantly swelled like balloons due to the force at which I was connecting it with but my own pain had gone deeper than that.

"Come on you fucker" as I grabbed a head full of hair and dragged it out onto the landing.

WHACK!! there's another just for good luck.

"Down the stairs with you my beauty!" I yelled and off it went tumbling like a stunt man (or was that woman or something).

I threw it's clothing down the stairs and was at the bottom of the stairs myself in about three strides.

"Here's one more you sad fucker" and with that launched a beauty into it. I opened the front door; picked it up and helped it on its way out, threw the clothing out and slammed the door.

Shit!

Did I slam that door;

the whole fucking glass came out!

"If I fucking see you again"! I shouted whilst pointing through what was now basically a door with no glass.

**"MMm, don't worry, you will"** (said Kenneth Williams).

Meanwhile.......... There in the living room, is Stu and Dusty.

The settee has now gone over backwards and these two have gone with it. All I can see is two pairs of legs that are waving about in the air like the robotic things from the Cadbury Potato Smash advert that we all enjoyed so many years ago on T.V. and they have pissed themselves whilst laughing Kit-bags!! The cider flagon is rolling around with them and I want an excuse!

"You knew didn't you, you fuckers!" as I looked over the settee at them both, faces absolutely soaked with tears of laughter.

"Well?"

**"Fuck me son...yeh we knew,"** (still bawling with laughter) said Stuart.

**"I was only going to share a taxi with her man"** Fucking HER, I thought!

**"Yeh, it lives just round the corner and I thought it would be cheaper for me to share".**

"What, you've done it before?" I asked.

**"WHY I MAN"** he replied.

"So, how comes you didn't tell me then, when I fucked off in the taxi with it?"

**"Because you never asked, you greedy twat"** he said.

I'd travelled quite a bit when I was in the Navy and knew of the tell-tale signs to look out for when in areas such as Hamburg or the Far East. Never in my wildest dreams did I think I would get caught in the Somerset town of Yeovil. You know, quaint little surrounding villages with cottages and the like.

But, there you go.........all part of growing up I suppose. Stuart didn't realize that my time would come.............it was now game-on!

# COW HILL AND THE PENNY FLUTES

"Let's go outside, sit in a circle and play our penny flutes," said Ido.

"Wait a minute, Horace is asleep and he's pissed himself" I said

"and look, I think Stu is up to one of his tricks".

Horace had indeed fallen asleep and being as drunk as he was, could not control his bladder. The trouble was, was that we were sat in the Launderette right next to the town bus station at about 5p.m. on a busy Saturday afternoon, with nothing on but white cotton bed sheets that the owner of the place had given us to cover ourselves up in.

You see, about ten of us had been out for a Saturday lunch time session and we had all met at around 11a.m. in the Greyhound pub (very popular in it's day). Camp was boring during the weekend and if you were not a weekend traveller, like taking your dirty washing home to mummy or going to see your loved one, then a full day session was pretty much on the cards. Anyway, we sat down and talked about the usual shite…. football, girls, girls, and football. A bunch of young, free lads just having a beer or two.

**"All reet man Ali, so you've just farted next to me, now piss-off and leave me hair alone"** ranted Stuart.

Stuart was sat with his back to the toilets and didn't see Ali walking towards him with a little gift. The rest of us just sat there with quirky smiles as Ali began to rub it into Stu`s hair like some sort of conditioner.

"Must have had a bad pint last night and there's no bog- paper in there" replied Ali. Holy Moses, he did stink! Stuart being Stuart was straight on the defensive and made his way to the bogs.

"Christ" I thought, "we've only had a pint and the malarkey has started already".

It wasn't long before Stu returned with about 2lbs. of `Slack-Hampton` cupped in his hand and he was heading straight for us!

"Hold on a minute Stu, we're going to get thrown out of here if this carries on" said one of the lads.

"Pop it in the payout slot of the fruit machine if you want a laugh". So off he strolled over to the machine and sneakily deposited it into the winnings slot. The pub was relatively empty, as it not long had opened so we had the bar and staff to ourselves knowing that within an hour the place would be heaving. Stu had returned from washing his hands and came back to sit down via the bar with 2 double Pernod & Coke. He liked a drop of Pernod with his pint did Stuart.

Well time was cracking on and the ale was flowing at a rapid rate. Stuart was now awash with Pernod and obviously on a mission to drink the pub dry of it.

**"Check oot the lasses at the froot machine lads"** he said. In went the £1 and around went the spools. We all watched from about 20 feet where we were sat...nothing. Around they went again.........
Result! Click, click, click went the machine as it paid out the winnings.

Another £1 goes in, around go the spools...Result!

Click, click, click went the winnings but strangely enough no sound of coins collecting in the tray. Stuart meanwhile has remembered his pint that is now about an hour old and is flat as a witch's tit. **"Ya durty bastads"** he hollows **"Who the fuck`s done this!!!!!!!!!!!"** He's got something strange hanging half in and half out of his mouth. Everyone is now in fits of laughter and just to make matters worse, the gambling queens have decided to collect their winnings but are now hysterical as one of them has a couple of lbs. of Stuarts dodder all over her hands.

The girls run screaming to the toilets and Stuart makes a beeline to the fruit machine. In an instant, we all got up and were making our way quickly for the door when a couple asked if we had finished sitting here.

"Yeh, help yourselves" we said, Stuart obviously thought we were still sat there and with a rapid twist of his body at the same time launching his arm as though he was bowling a cricket ball, lobbed a gift from the fruit machine towards the table.

His face was a picture and the couples face that of horror as this projectile span through the air. We had got about two or three steps out of the door when we heard,

"Oi you, come here", Stuart came bounding out the door with the owner in hot pursuit. Every man for himself as this bloke was pretty tasty, it didn't take us long to lose him.

**"Ya wankers ya, he could have given me a gud hiding back there man,"** panted Stuart.

"Do you think we would have left you? Come on, you've had enough shit for today…literally" I said, let's get in here.

We had doubled back on ourselves and went across the road from the Greyhound to a pub called The Globe & Crown, notorious for its pints of Cider and Vimto and its clientele of biker gangs. The bikers must have been busy elsewhere this particular day as we had the `Office` all to ourselves.

The `Office` was a room just off to the side of the pub away from prying eyes and the like with it's own little serving hatch straight through to the bar. Our favorite pastime in here apart from drinking cider was that renowned game of `Snuff Buzz`. We would sit around a table and someone would start by saying

"To my right….7" the person on his right then had to reply with…8 on his right…9 and so on until the figure had a 7 in it or was a multiple of 7(for example 14). Rather than that person saying 14, he would say BUZZ and the game would continue with 15 but in the opposite direction, until someone ballsed-up. Sounds easy, but with numerous pints on board, it can be quite difficult or you can make out as though you are just fucking thick!

That person would then have to undergo the dreaded snuff!

Jez always seemed to be in charge of the snuff and made sure that you got a good heap of it on your fist. Count to 3 and up the old nostrils it goes! Just another little pastime that gave us a laugh, there would soon be some right states sat around the table. Time was getting on and Idris commented that because it was such a lovely day, we should be sat outside.

"Let's go to Peter Dominic's (off-license) get ourselves a carry-out and go up to `cow hill` eh?" he said.

We all agreed and finished off our Cider. Having bought our liquid refreshment, we headed for Tescos to buy cheese and French sticks but on the way, someone thought it be a good idea to pop into the musical instrument shop at the bottom of town and buy some tin penny flutes,

why?

I don't know but soon everyone became the Pied Piper of ye olde Yeovil town. Cheese and French sticks, flagons of cider and tin flutes, surely we could entertain ourselves for the rest of the afternoon up on cow hill.

`Cow Hill` was named as such because there were always cows roaming freely around the hill hence,

`cow hill`

and overlooked the whole town as it is of some size. Having staggered half way up the hill we sat down and made ourselves comfortable. No sooner had we sorted ourselves out came a rush of blood to the head from someone.

**"Who fancies trying to ride the cows' man?"**

`Fuck me` I thought,

we now have a budding Rodeo cowboy in our midst! You got it in one again…Stuart.

Not only were we topped up with ale and still topping up, but we are now sat on a hill that had a 30 degree slope on it and was covered in cowshit, not to mention that no-one had passed their cow riding course that I knew of and Stuart wants to ride cows!

Everyone looked at one another, paused, and then stood up to choose their favorite steed.

"Stuart, do you really want to try this?"

I asked, for the simple reason he was in one hell of a state.

**"Ya don't know `Jack Shitt` son!** (See next chapter) **"Just watch this, I've been to a Rodeo when I was in the States and av seen how it's done man"** and at that proceeded to chase after this huge cow.

"Go on Stu, go on mate", came the encouragement from the lads. Stuart managed to make this cow turn up hill, that slowed it down a bit and this gave `Wild Bill Hickock` half a chance to launch himself onto its back.

So here we are, looking at this crazed Geordie who is full of Pernod now hanging on for dear life on the back of a cow which has now turned down hill and is having none of this. He must have lasted about 10 seconds when the cow ejected him straight onto numerous piles of cowshit. Off he went sliding down the hill on his arse collecting cowpats as he went. The lads were in fits of laughter and a few of them decided they would show him how it was done. Needless to say, every one of them ended up with the same result as Stuart and those who were still sat there merrily taking in the entertainment, were bombarded with cowpats, the majority of them still fresh!

Time-out.

Time for refreshment. Looking around at each other we realized that we smelled as bad as the cows. We had planned to stay in town all day and carry on straight into the night. What with it being during the summer months, the night life started quite early in the evening in town and we were going to be part of it.

"I suppose we better go and order some taxis back to camp eh?" said Ali

"What for?" we queried

"Well, to get cleaned up and get out of this shitty gear ready for tonight" he replied.

"£11 for a taxi!! You must be fucking joking, we'll get sorted out in town here, come on lets get to the launderette" I said.

So off we trudged down `cow hill` and through the bottom end of town to the launderette, looking like we had just done a hard days graft on a farm! The launderette was right next to the main bus station and it was packed with shoppers waiting for their respective buses.

**"Haway man, let's gan in and get this sorted oot, who's putting his gear in with mine then"?** Stuart asked,

"WE ALL WILL" was our reply and at that we all stripped off and bunged our gear in the washing machine. Plenty of soap powder and off we go. Looking back on it all, we probably could have made a mint on T.V. as this was happening about 6 or 7 years before the Levis Jeans advert where the bloke strips down to his undies in the launderette and washes his jeans!

With everyone else in there looking on. So anyway, that's when the owner came down stairs and saw us sat there quietly, looking as though nothing was wrong apart from the fact that it was 5:00 on a Saturday afternoon and we were sat in our knicks and socks.

"Jesus"! You can't sit in here like that fellas, here, put these round you" as the owner passed us several white cotton bed sheets from behind his counter.

"Well, this is a first for me" he said, as he stood there stunned.

**"Div` nt worry mate, give us an hour and we'll be oota here, ya see it happened like this"** and off went Stuart explaining how we come to be half naked.

"Come on, let's go outside, sit in a circle and play our penny flutes," said Idris.

"You never know, we might even make a few coins and it will pass the time".

"Wait a minute, Horace is asleep and he's pissed himself and look I think Stu is up to one of his tricks," I said, as we were walking out into the bus station entrance.

Sure enough, Stuart was up to something as usual.

Horace was absolutely out of it, snoring his head off whilst laid at the back of the launderette on a wooden slated bench with one of these cotton sheets draped over him. The owner has now gone through to the back and `you know who` has lifted up the sheet that's draped over Horace.

Stuart runs his penny flute from left to right across his lips whilst lubricating it with his tongue and without any fuss at all, inserts it up Horace's jacksee!!  Not a whimper came from Horace as Stuart slowly but surely looses his flute, twisting it as he went.  Our sides are splitting with laughter what with one thing then another and I'm wondering when it's all going to stop.

About 4 or 5 had congregated outside and were sat in a circle cross-legged with the sheets wrapped around them trying to serenade the `shopping bag laden ladies` with their penny flutes! It actually worked. People were walking past and throwing coins into the middle of the circle, they must have thought that they were one of these musical groups that travel around town centers and set up an instrument playing session.I could just picture an old lady asking if they sold any tapes of there haunting musical sounds!

The washing is nearly finished and all being well, we should have our jeans in the dryer any minute we thought. Oh No!!!! Stuart has decided to try and play his flute in the launderette and you know what is been blown out of every hole in the flute and now there's pandemonium in the place!

The owner is doing his nut! He's emptied the washing machine and we are now ejected with sodden wet jeans on.

"divint worry man lads, at least we divint smell like farmers anymore and the neet is only beginning" Stuart said, whilst laughing Kit-bags!!

# WHO THE HELL IS JACK SHITT?

(Jack Shitt)  Commonly said throughout the forces to one-another meaning: you don't know nothing, zero, zilch, fuck-all, not-a-clue, etc.

## <u>SO</u>

Jack is the only son of Awe Shitt and O` Shitt. Awe Shitt is a fertilizer manufacturer and is a partner in Kneedeep & Shitt incorporated.  In turn, Jack Shitt married Noe Shitt and the deeply religious couple produced six children: Wholly Shitt, Fuller Shitt, Giver Shitt, Bull Shitt, and the twins Deap and Dip Shitt. Against her parents objections, Deap married her cousin, Dumb Shitt who himself was a high school dropout! After 15 years of marriage the parents divorced and Noe Shitt later on married a guy called Mr. Sherlock, but because of her kids still living with her she wanted to keep her previous surname, therefore being known as Noe Shitt Sherlock.  Dip Shitt married Loda Shitt and together had a wonderful son named Chicken.  Fuller Shitt and Giver Shitt were inseparable throughout childhood and subsequently married the Happens brothers. The wedding announcement in the local newspaper told of the Shitt-Happens wedding. Bull Shitt, the prodigal son who left home to tour the world and educate himself returned some years later with his new bride who was originally from Italy and was named Pizza Shitt. So now, if someone says that "You don't know Jack Shitt", you can correct them and say with confidence that.......................................... Not only do you know Jack Shitt but you know all the rest of the family too!!

# NO CHRISTMAS LEAVE

Christmas leave would soon be upon us and everyone was looking forward to getting home for a while with families and no doubt quaffing large amount of ale with their mates back home, everyone apart from me and Stuart that is! We had a spell of Commanders Punishment leading up to Christmas leave and the money situation didn't look good at all so as everyone was preparing to bog-off for two weeks, we acknowledged the fact that we would be having Traditional Christmas lunch with the Duty Watch. Stuart at the time leading up to our reprimanding was employed as Mess-Man in the Senior Rates Mess (a cushy number in anyone's book). Basically looking after the Mess for the Seniors whilst they were at work, delivering newspapers, making sure the hot water urn was topped up, getting mail, etc. General dogs-body with some good perks like playing snooker every day, reading newspapers, and if you were good at it you would work behind the Mess bar at lunch times (which obviously had its own perks!).

I myself was employed on the `Buffers Party`. Basically, we were the `Wombles` of the whole Establishment, cleaning up everyone else's crap and litter along with a few other menial tasks. It was one of the sections you could join whilst waiting for your time to go back to front-line squadrons. I wont knock it too much though as it also had its share of perks. One of which was buying the Christmas trees for the whole of the Establishment (of which we would sell at a profit of-course) All the `Buffers` lads would put in around £50 each and off to the local forestry we would go in our wagon with around £500 (and our wood saws). The forestry commission guy would do us a deal and whilst loading up the trees from an already pile of them, a couple of lads would sneak into the densely populated area and cut trees down like they were going out of fashion!

All loaded up (with our freebie trees as well) we would wish the forestry guy a Merry Christmas and be on our way back to the Camp. The trees were sized and priced accordingly and a message would be put on Daily Orders that the `Buffers Party` were holding their annual tree sell off.

It was like selling sweets to kids!!

The Captains Office obviously got the best tree out of the lot of them, to which we had a `Well-Done` from his secretary….the rest was first come-first served. It goes without saying that we all made our initial deposit back with more than enough money to give ourselves a bloody good Christmas drink for all our hard work. Stuart had been invited to our lunchtime drinks party and so we locked up the store having squared everything away as we were officially now on Christmas leave.

All ticketyboo, off we went to the Houndstone bar. A bar which was about 10 mile away from camp situated inside a disused Army camp but now being used for military transport and stores. A quiet place out of the way of prying eyes which was just as well!!!!! The Commander had given my boss at the time, John Anderson, an ultimatum, which I was allowed to go for our Christmas drink on the condition that he tied himself to me with a length of 6 foot x 2 inch thick manila rope!!

What did he think I was going to do? Run away from free fucking beer!!

The afternoon went along brilliantly with the usual bar games along with copious amount of ale and as the time was rolling along, so were johns' eyes! It wasn't long before he was sound asleep with his head on the bar-top.

**"How much is left in the kitty pet?"** asked Stuart to the bar girl. "Not much, you've just about done the lot and its only 3 o'clock"!! She replied.

**"Howay man, a know where we can go an av a gud time man, a know this lass who'll see us alreet"** Stuart said, looking cross-eyed through his milk-bottle bottomed glasses.

**"Hurry up man before her kids get outa skool".** So, undoing the rope, I left John there sleeping and wished the rest of the lads a good leave. About half an hour later after staggering around these streets we finally found Stuarts destination.

**"Reet son, let me dee the talking and the ground work and then afta aboot 15 minutes come up and get stuck in, alreet"** said Stuart.

No problem I thought….knowing you Stuart it wouldn't surprise me if she was a Transvestite or something so yes please, be my guest!

We were welcomed at the door by Stuart's friend and

went into her sitting room whereupon I clocked my eyes on two kids, one about 4 and the other about 7.

**"Now then, ya uncle Ditchy is gona tell ya a story while me and ya mam av a chat aboot old times"** said Stuart to the kids. I found myself trying to read Goldilocks and the 3 bears whilst being shitters!!

God knows how much I construed that story; anyway the kids seemed to enjoy it. Lover boy was now upstairs thinking he was some kind of porn star by the noises that was coming from the bedroom, so I finished the story along with the half bottle of Bacardi I had found in the kitchen and got the kids to go and play Goldilocks in the back garden. Stripping my gear off as I went up the stairs, ol` matey-boy was at it hammer and tongs! Wearing nothing but a smile I was greeted by the Italian Stallion himself at the top of the stairs.

**"What ya dooin man.....not yet man"** said Stuart blocking the doorway.

"I've come for a look first man" I replied.

**"Well me old` mate.......Look at this"**!! And with that give me a beauty right on the good night button! Off I went head over arse down the stairs! To him laughing his fucking head off! Minutes had passed when I finally came round with him standing over me trying to wake me up. He had obviously done his deed with madam and it was now time to leave but I was looking like a baby unicorn with this fucking great golf ball of a lump on my forehead and my top lip split right through! Laughing his head off at me I quipped that I would have the last laugh and that I would be filing it with the rest of the shit I owed him!

The night went much like any other night in town

apart from that I had to drink my pints through a fucking straw! Because my top lip was flapping about! Having visited hospital and got sorted and stitched we went back to camp.

The following day saw everyone going their respective ways on Christmas leave.

**"Reet, lets get round all the cabins and see if anyone has left and shrapnel (coins) aboot and we'll go for a drink in the men's bar eh"?** Said Stuart. This was the duty bar on camp over a main leave period. We managed to rustle up enough to buy a crate of Newcastle Brown Ale (24 bottles of it). Sat at a table in the bar everyone was in their subdued mode because they were duty and wanted to be home.

Me and boyo?

Well we just got on with our crate thinking the quicker we neck this, the quicker we will fall asleep and another 24 hours will be over! All of a sudden, in came the duty Regulator (military copper). On looking round he saw that me and Stuart were enjoying ourselves a little too much and told us to stop drinking and that we had to leave the bar! Mistake number 1!!! No-one would stop us drinking especially one of the Reg` staff who had gone out of their way to make sure we had been seriously fined over the top for something trivial but this is how they got there kicks by seeing guys not being able to go on leave because they had no money to. Don't get me wrong, if caught in the act of disobeying rules then you have to suffer the consequences but these guys loved there job a bit too much! It was bad enough when the `Fleet Master At Arms` had ordered us to go and represent `The Crows` (his pet name for us young blooded, full spirited, work hard play hard lads) at the Christmas Carole Service! Not that I have anything against the Carole service at all…. it was just the way that the narrow-minded Regulators thought they would be-little us in front of our mates! We both went though which was a surprise to the Captain and his fellow Officers and sung our hearts out!!!

Anyway, back in the bar I'm sat trying to reason with the duty regulator, when out of the corner of my eye I see Stuart with a fully charged fire hose pointing right at our friend!

"Sorry, I really do need to rush to the bog" and up and off I was. I managed to get about three or four steps away when about 200 p.s.i. of water come winging over the room hitting the regulator smack in the middle of his chest sending him flat up against the wall!!! The place was in up raw!! And at the end of the hose was fireman Sam!! In fits of laughter!

**"Everyman for himself"** shouted Stuart as he threw the hose to the ground. It wasn't long before people were sliding all over the place and running for the door, a charged hose flying around is something you do not want to be near. I was out the door like a flash, around the corner and into the NAFFI Automat (drinks, sandwiches, etc).

"Stan, Aye up, what's goin on?" asked Knoppy.

I quickly briefed him on what Stu had got up to and sat myself in a corner of the automat, Stuart didn't take long to come bursting through the door!

**"Its alreet man, the Reggie as gone the other way lookin for us, I'll just gan back n' get our crate of Ale"** he says. He obviously went back to his cabin to clean up because we sat there with

Knoppy and seen off the rest of the crate! By now we were well on the way (once again) and Stuart was feeling worse for wear!

**"I'm off to get me heed down, give az a shake at aboot 7 o'clock man"** he slurred. As he left the automat, Knoppy and I saw him collapse to the ground with a thud. On getting outside we realized that Stuart had definitely had his fill of Newcastle Brown and was snoring his head off within seconds!

"Come on Stan, lets get him to bed" said knoppy (who himself by the way, was still on Commanders punishment over Christmas leave. His punishment was to be in No 1s uniform from the minute he woke until he went to bed in the Guardroom, mustering at the Guardroom every 2 hours, every day of the leave period....the imbugerance of it all!)

"Just hold on a minute Knoppy, theres a little pay back time due for our Stuart me old mate" I said with an `I said I would have the last laugh` sound to my reply.

Not forgetting, we had just consumed a crate of Newcastle Brown Ale, also not forgetting all the ale we had yesterday. Well, my guts were churning up real bad and yep, you got it........ Down came the jeans and Stuarts head became the proud owner of about 3lbs of `slack-Hampton`!!! Knoppy just stood in amazement as I'm sure one would, but you see, unless you gave Stuart as good if not better than he could dish out, then he would try and try to better you.... I knew that he wouldn't be able to better this!! Hahahahahahaha!

"**Now...** we'll put him to bed" I replied to Knoppy who was stood in the corner of the door way retching.

"No fucker whacks me down stairs and gets away with it, nor lets me tap up his transvestite mates without warning me, come on give me a hand to pick him up"

I could see why Knoppy was a bit hesitant but even I couldn't leave him there, so off to Collingwood block we dragged him and plonked him down on his bed. About 5 hours later…all I heard was

**"You dirty, dirty bastard! You filthy, dirty bastard!"**

"Oh, that'll be our Stuart awake then" and as I got up from my bed in a cabin down the corridor I waited and watched for him coming out of his cabin. I dropped to my knees in a fit of laughter as I was looking at something out of a 1950s Alfred Hitchcock scary movie! Never in my life have I seen anything as funny. There was laughing boy, stood naked with a bed pillow stuck to the side of his head! His face looked like he had used a mud-pack from the Serengeti Plains! In 5 hours his new face-pack had dried well and truly.

I was in hysterics!!
**"I divint know what you're laughing at, ya gona av to wash Taffs bedding".**
I only put him down on the wrong bed hadn't I?

A menial task I thought compared to the one you are about to go through…..Wonder how long it will take you to peel your face-pack off? And off to the showers he trudged hahahahahahahaahahaha! PRICELESS.

I stood there laughing Kit-bags!!

My old time buddy, Stu Foss hung-over at work!

Left to Right: Chesh,Mac,Graham,Frenchy,
Crash,Danny,Bob,Ross,Topsy,
Alfie,The Author kneeling at
back,Paddy,Jack,Chris,Jumper
`If only Carlsberg made Flights! `

`Just sitting around in the desert! `

`The Stranglers` having a photo call with the bar staff of
`D Flight` seniors just prior to party time. Bosnia.

The Author, Harry and Alex.
Bardufoss B-B-Q. Norway. Its -20 degrees outside!

Dressed for `Burns Night` in the Seniors bar, Bardufoss,
Norway. `Don't know what the guy in the sunglasses is
up to`!

Dressed for braveheart night, downtown Bardufoss…
Weapons handed in to Night-Club doorman!! Wonder
why?

`The Curry Club`. Bosnia.

`Honest` Ron Wilson and the Author enjoying a beer in Kuwait.

Myself with Kate Aide (BBC war correspondent) in our tent somewhere in the Saudi desert during Gulf war 1. I decided to make a trifle for her using ingredients mainly from a 24 hr food ration pack. Bless her; she tried her best to eat it, washed down with `Swan` non-alcoholic lager, nice!! The trifle can be seen on the table.

# YANKIE CHARLIE,
# YANKIE CHARLIE

"How's about I organize a trip to the North East eh"? I said to Dave Ringrow who was our Manpower controller on 845 Squadron and once the young cockney lad who bunked next to me when we first joined up. Remember? Him with the biscuits.

"Pick your team then and find a pilot willing to fly for you and don't forget to run it by the boss" was his reply.

Well that was easy enough I thought.

"Oh, and by the way, I want to come and you can only do it during summer leave" he added as I was leaving the office.

Now I knew a lot of the lads would be going home for the leave period but I also knew that a few of them would forsake a long week-end for a visit to the North East! As it happens it was the fellas I had in mind to crew the trip, about 8 of us in total...all hand-picked fun guys who you could rely on at work and at play!

"Sir, OK if I organize a trip to the North East next week-end, got the crew, sorted the accommodation, got all the logistics and spares, all we need is a pilot and

102

aircrewman" I asked with a pleasing smile on my face as I stood in the doorway of the Senior pilots office.

"Cant see that being a problem, make sure you fill out the necessary paperwork and I want to see something on it that will justify your weekend away" he replied.

"No problem Sir".

All I've got to do now is ask around the pilots to see who wants to fly the helicopter.

"I would love to do it" said ................(No way can I name him when writing this as he is still serving and I would hate any repercussions for him as he is without doubt one of the best Officer/bloke and pilot I have come across). So we will call him Lt. Good-guy for this story.

So gear packed, aircraft cleared for maintenance all the weekend, fully fuelled, let's get it on!!

Oh, by the way, the paperwork had been cleared for us to go as I had set up a 'wet water exercise' involving the lifeboat crew operating in Sunderland. They were obviously delighted that we were travelling up from Somerset to do some sea drills with them and to strengthen my request, had also organized for us to drop in at my old school in Sunderland to show off the Helicopter (that's another story!!). All that plus the fact that the pilot and his aircrew man (Mac) could practice various flying objectives on the way up (low-level, map reading, etc)....any excuse!!

We finally arrived at our destination and got everything squared away. The city of Newcastle was calling and it didn't take us long to get our glad-rags on and hit the town. The night went along as planned, all the fellas making out that they were Navy helicopter pilots and that Lt Good guy was our `Steward` who had been brought along to make us breakfast and polish our boots!!!

Late that night we ended up on the Tuxedo Princess, an old P & O Ferry that has been tied up on Newcastle quay side for years and turned into a nightclub with numerous themed bars. Lt. Good-guy was at the bar getting his round of drinks in when I decided once and for all that I was going to let everyone in the bar know who was the pilot.

"Give me a shot of your microphone please mate" I asked the guy who was playing a big white piano.

"Why? You going to give us a song? He asked.

"Nope, but check this out" I said.

"Right then party people......Contrary to what you may have been told tonight by these Navy lads...don't believe them...I'm the pilot of that helicopter (parked not 200 yards behind the back of the boat) and if you want a flight then I want you all at the main gate outside there at 10am tomorrow alright?"

Silence, then.........YAHOO!!

Screaming, whistling, clapping... fuck-me, the place erupted. All these free drinks were getting passed around the lads and in the corner of the bar was Lt. Good-guy with that (what the fuck have you said) look on his face hahaha!

Now of course, everyone wanted to know the Navy lads and there was some quality stories' going around, the best I think was....

"I bet you didn't think you would meet a Navy dolphin trainer tonight eh?" as one of the lads try to impress this group of girls.

"I've got to listen to this one I thought"

"Yeah, course I do. The dolphins are captured and flown from America whereupon I train them down at Portsmouth to track Russian submarines with sonar collars around their heads and then I release them just off the coast of Scotland. They swim around protecting our shores whilst sending back signals to Intelligence HQ".

The group of lasses just stood with their mouths open, absolutely astonished!! And so did I!! Unfuckingbelieveable I thought! And had to walk away before I pissed myself laughing.

Morning came and we were woken up by the shouts of

**"Haway then you Navy lads, where's the pilot then"**? Lt. Good-guy said "I think they are asking for you `Biggles`" as he grinned from his sleeping bag. At that I got some gear on and went outside the building whereupon I was greeted by about 20 lads and lasses!!!

"I'm sorry but we can't fly today, we have to sort the engines out. You see, last night a Seagull got into one of the engine exhausts and got himself stuck…it's a right mess and we have to sort it out, so sorry about that, I really am".

"Can we stand here and take photographs then?" one asked.

"Help yourself love, it's the least I can do for you", and at that I was off back to my sleeping bag!!

"Sort it out then `Biggles`, did you? Said Lt.Good-guy.

"I, I did that. Now let's get back to sleep eh".

We had lunch and got the helicopter ready for our rendezvous with the Sunderland lifeboat crew out in the North Sea somewhere.

There's two seats in the cockpit of a helicopter, one for the pilot (obviously) and the other for the co-pilot. Lt. Good-guy was obviously flying the thing and I was given the opportunity to sit in the co-pilots seat, (a common practice if there is no co-pilot with you and the seat is available). Mac was in the back doing his aircrewman thing, pre-flight checks, running the winch cable out making sure there was no snags, and contacting the coxswain of the lifeboat over the radio to find his position. Everything ticketyboo, off we went. Flying out over the North Sea everything was as normal, weather was good. Visibility was good as we could see for miles. The plan was to home in on a signal from a distress beacon which a lifeboat crew member would have whilst he was sat in a dingy that was bobbing around in the North Sea, hover above him and winch him up out of the dingy, radio the main lifeboat that we had him onboard and then find the lifeboat and winch him down onto it.

Simple.

This went on for quite some time, winching up and down, flying round and around but the North Sea being what it is can change in the blink of an eye and didn't it fucking just do that!

Within minutes the weather changed around us.

The sea had a good swell on it now and the wind had picked up considerably. As it happens we were flying around ready to winch up our last lifeboat guy. "About half a mile on your left boss" said Mac. Lt.Good-guy banked the helicopter over we had sight of him in front of us.

"Haway lets get there, the poor fuckers getting thrown about something rotten" said Mac through his helmet microphone.

106

Hovering about 100 feet, Mac gave precise directions to Lt. Good-guy and brought the helicopter close to the dingy.

"Another 10 feet right, touch more,right,steady there boss, winch going down now, hold it there" Mac said to Lt. Good-guy who was keeping the helicopter on a pin-point considering the fucking North East winds were battering shit out of us.

"On the winch, bringing him up now" instructed Mac.

Lt. Good-guy keeping the helicopter in a perfect hover and me looking over my shoulder from the cockpit to see the last guy being winched up into the helicopter.

"FUCK!! IVE LOST HIM" shouted Mac.

And at that Lt. Good guy started to pull power and bank the helicopter around at a fucking great angle.

WHACK, WHACK, WHACK….. was the noise of the main rotor blades as he did a circuit to go around and winch up the crew member who had fallen into the North Sea!!

Or so we thought.

The tendency when being winched up or down from a helicopter is that you want to lift your arms up and grab the cable that you are on the end of (bad idea).

All users are briefed fully before use that when being winched your arms are to be crossed in front of your body whilst in the winching strop……lift them up and you will drop through the strop!! So there we were doing about 80 knots and about 80 feet, banking the helicopter over to get around and pick this guy up quick when all of a sudden we heard over the VHF radio in a strong Sunderland accent................

"YANKEE CHARLIE, YANKEE CHARLIE, YA DRAGGIN HIM THROUGH THE FUCKIN WATER MAN".

It was the coxswain of the lifeboat who was watching one of his crew being body surfed through the North Sea on the end of a helicopters winch cable!!

What Mac said was "I've lost him" both Lt Good-guy and myself thought the obvious, that he had lifted his arms up and slipped out of the winch strop.

What Mac really meant to say was "I've lost SIGHT of him.

The wind was that strong it had blown him to a position which was out of Macs sight under the aircraft while he was winching him up. When we realized what was going on, Lt Good-guy came to a hover and Mac continued to winch up the lifeboat member. It had all happened in a space of about 20 seconds, not long but long enough to see that the guys face was like a smacked arse, with sea-weed hanging out of his wet-suit. Mac pulled him into the helicopter cabin and broke down in laughter.

The guys face was a picture.

He had taken on about 6 gallon of North Sea inside his wet-suit but give him his due......He was also laughing Kit-bags!! That night we all met up with the lifeboat crew and had a bloody good laugh along with well earned ale........The surfer took 3 days off work!!

# ANYONE FOR DINNER?

The crew had been picked and we were off to Kinloss in Scotland to do some anti-terrorist drills with the SBS (Special Boat Service).

We were to stay at RAF Kinloss but when we arrived we were told that there wasn't enough accommodation for us on the camp and so we would have to book into a hotel near by (shit eh?).

Kinloss would supply transport for us to get to and from work to the hotel every day for the rest of the detachment. (Thank you). The week went as planned and the SBS got to do their thing. Day in day out we would pick them up and fly out to designated oil rigs off Kinloss whereupon the helicopter would do a tactical maneuver and allow the SBS to drop onto the rig and carry out their drills

So, like I said the week went on and so did the evenings in the local pub. Well, there's fuck all else to do in Kinloss believe me!!!! We were welcomed each evening by a group of WRAF girls from the camp in this same boozer so we thought we would exchange a few words (as you do) and got on quite well with them.

"I know, lets have a detachment B-B-Q on Sunday at the hotel and we'll invite the lasses along eh?" I said.

"Right girls, you sort us out with a 12 man tent and all the B-B-Q cooking gear and we'll get the grub and the drink, yes?" I said.

"Sounds good to us" they replied......................
Game on!! Sunday came and the place was set up on the lawn just to the side of the hotel we were staying at. The owner said we could enjoy ourselves and that she didn't mind as we had behaved ourselves all week and gave her no grief.....as if we would. Coals were lit, music is on, beer is flowing and the sun is shining. Had a good weeks work out of us, time to relax and enjoy!

"Here comes the tottie" shouts Bob as the girls arrived in our transport of course that had been kindly given to us by the camp for our duration in Kinloss.

"Here you are girls, get stuck in, there's enough drink for everyone, grub will be ready soon" said Minnie, our duty chef.

Music was blasting out, beer being quaffed, laughter all round...good times.

"Aye up, where's whats-her-name, you know the one with the massive chest"? Asks Bob to one of the girls.

"She's got up late and will make her own way here" says her mate, shouldn't be long". Bob went back to the cool bin for another beer. About 2 hours later or so I realized that Harry had gone missing and went to look to see if he had got his head down in his hotel room. Opened the door, no-one there but his balcony window was open. On looking out I nearly fell over the balcony railings for there on the gravel car-park was the girl with the massive chest sat in a MGBGT sports car with the roof down, fast asleep! So I was on my way back to the B-B-Q when I was met by Gaz just outside the foyer.

"Anyone for dinner"? Asks Gaz.

"What the fuck are you on about" I said.

"Come with me and see what I've found" he says, giggling like a fucking little school-boy! Turning the corner onto the gravel drive he pointed at the MGBGT car....

"Look, it's her, the one with the superb tits and she's out for the count" beamed Gaz.

And at that made a bee-line straight for the car without a care in the world.

"Hold on, what do ya mean, she's out for the count"?

"She's pissed right up isn't she and she's only driven herself here". "Look" as he grabbed one of her tits...

"she's fucking away with the fairies" he says.

She was snoring a lot and stank of ale!

"Aye up lets get one of these beauties out eh" as he popped his hand down her top and lobbed out the biggest tit I've ever seen.

"Jesus...says Gaz, fuck me its heavy...lets see if the other weighs the same eh"?

Out came the other one and there she was in all her majesty!!!! She never budged or moved a bit........

"Right then...I'm not letting these beauties go to waste" says Gaz as he leans over the driver's door and nuzzles onto her tit like a hungry baby!

"You having the other or what then"? He didn't need to prompt me twice and I was soon in the passenger side and locked onto her other tit like another hungry baby!

Jesus!! she must have had some drink as she never moved an inch!! "PISST...PISST"...over here..

Minnie was sat on a dwarf wall having a smoke watching me and Gaz having our dinner.

"Fellas, just keep on sucking on them lovely tits but raise your eyes sideways and have a look at this" suggested Minnie.

The whole world went into slow motion.........

for there looking at the 2 hungry babies was the whole fucking Hotel restaurant, having Sunday lunch!! The dining room couldn't have had bigger windows!!!!!!!!!!!!! Kids were getting a slap around the head and so were a lot of husbands too. Tits were restored to there resting place. Gaz and I bowed to our audience and calmly walked away to rapturous applause from male dinners who were still receiving slaps around the head!!!! Minnie sat there laughing Kit-bags!!

# GOING DOWN

The dits` you have just read are in no particular dated order, they were just a few experiences I had over my first 12 years in the Navy and trust me, theres a lot more!

Looking back, my early years were a bit up and down in the fact that, one month I would be in the shit…the next; I would be knuckling down and staying out of trouble.

It was like that for **all of us**. Why? Because even though it was a disciplined time, it was also a case of `work hard, play hard, play harder! `**All of us**` consisted of about 15 guys (some of them with WRNS hanging off their arms) but anyway, everyone got on well and looked out for one-another. As time went by `we` were branded with the name B.B.C. (no-doubt from some good guy or guys who didn't see the fun side in a bit of Horse-play!!). This so-called B.B.C. name was to stick with us for ages…..and I fucking hated it!! `Bad Boys Club` is what it meant!! Bad Boys? They didn't have a fucking clue!

We were not bad at all….Yes we were boisterous. Yes we liked drinking. Yes we had wild parties and girls in our accommodation. Yes we stripped off naked anywhere, anytime. Yes we had food fights in the junior rates galley.

Yes we raided WRNS quarters early hours in the morning with Gas masks on. Yes we had the MoD police earning there money. Yes we made a bit of money out of selling Christmas trees..............was that REALLY being BAD?...we also did our jobs 100% and some!!!

You lot know who you are and I really do hope you are reading this ... Some Naval Officers for your information get up to <u>exactly</u> the same things but for them it's called `High Spirits`! Well fuck-me!!! **We were Very High Spirited!!** During all my serving time though, If we made a place in a shit state from the effects of one of our parties, it was always cleaned up the following day better than what it was originally...............................

B.B.C...........MY ARSE!!!

Anyway, it all came to a head when we had made a visit to WRNS quarters one evening, about 1am, all of us with our Gas masks on (which would have frightened any fucker had you been sleeping at the time!). It was more of a `Lets see if we can get around WRNS quarters without getting caught challenge`.

Young, immature stuff really but at the time, a fucking good laugh! All was going well around the warren of cabins and messes. Some of the messes had up to 20 lasses asleep in them, all snoring, farting and the like!

In charge of the WRNS quarters was a Chief Wren named Annie Gaff. Whatever happens you did not want to be caught by her!! Fuck-me she was a Battle-axe! She would take no prisoners and would probably have given a quality right hook as well!

The challenge was just about over when Bren decided

he was going to have a little `Under the covers feel` of one of these sleeping beauties. "Everyman for himself" Shouts Bren.....the screams were fucking horrendous!! Light went on, girls were throwing things at us, screaming... absolute hell! Everyone made their own escape, not forgetting that this place is like a maze. You didn't need a dozen girls jumping on you because they would have held on at all costs only later to pass their catch over to Annie Gaff!!! We could here the dulcet tones of Annie as she bounded around the corridors.

"Who's in my fucking quarters" she bellowed!

`Fuck it` I thought, I'm getting in here.

I got into the shower & toilet area and hid myself in a toilet cubicle, closed the door.

My Gas mask went in the toilet, I put the seat down and squatted on up on the seat.

Trying hard to control my breathing I could hear lads been kicked to fuck from groups of girls whilst fighting their way out. As we all know, a crazed group of lasses are worse than blokes, more so if they think they have been groped in their beds whilst sleeping! The MoD police with dogs arrived within about 5 minutes.

"Fuck" I thought, "this is it now, lets go for one of the windows".

I got myself up onto a sink unit with half my body through the window. All of a sudden I had 6 stone of German Alsatian hanging off my trailing foot!!!

"Get down and I'll get him off "said this copper.

Gingerly, I got down.

"Just keep that fucking thing away from me" whilst pointing at some enraged hound just wanting to tuck into my fat arse! Annie Gaff was now stood at the entrance of the toilets with about 10 girls behind her wanting to get at me more than the fucking dog!

"It's not what you think it is Chief" I explained as I was ushered out and passed Annie and her girls. WHACK!! Annie landed me with one of her right hooks to the side of my head!

"I'll see you tomorrow young man" she scowled. P.C Plod escorted me up to the Guardroom whereupon I was given a wooden bed for the rest of the night and waited to see what punishment the morning would bring. Bren was occupying another cell with Dave in another and I had forgotten that my gasmask was still down a toilet!

Morning came and one-by-one we were summoned to see the `Joss-man` (Fleet Master at Arms) who tore the shit out of us!!!! I knew this would happen, so I briefed one of the lasses who used to hang around with us, that me and her were seeing each other, she phoned me to say that she had been summoned to the mans office and what was she to say? (He knew she frequented with us and thought she would blab it all out in front of him!).

Wrong!!

Had it been today, I would have sued him, due to the fact that while he was putting you in the picture his nose would be pressed against yours whilst shouting at the top of his voice! Fuck knows how much of his saliva I must have had in my mouth!!! God knows what he was passing on to me!!!

What this bloke's problem? All this shouting.

After the Joss-man had simmered down and got his blood pressure back to normal, I began with my excuse!

"Go on then `Slippery` (he called me slippery now and again as I always managed to slip out of his hands just when he thought he had me hahahahaha). I'm all fucking ears on this one, it better be good because this time, YOU my lad are GOING DOWN"!!

He directed at me with bulging red, horrible, eyes.

`Take it easy I thought or you might not live to see me go down`!

He was fucking trembling with rage, beads of sweat forming on his top lip. I was thinking, anytime now Jossman, you are going to have a heart attack!

"Well Sir"……. (big pause)…… "There I was minding my own business with my girlfriend standing at the Wailing Wall" (a wall that ran around the outside of WRNS quarters to keep lads like me out!).

"You see Sir, we had been to the Junior rates bar and had a good night (which was true) and because I know that there's a lot of fellas knocking about down around WRNS quarters, (His eyes start bulging again) I just had to make sure my girl was safely back at her accommodation and yes of course we had a kiss and cuddle outside" I explained with the face of an angel!

"So how were you found to be climbing out of a fucking shithouse window then in the quarters"!! He yelled.

"Sir"…….my girl and I were frightened when we saw the MoD police running our way with dogs, so would you have been Sir" I quipped.

"DON'T –YOU- FUCKIN –TELL- ME-WHAT-I–WOULD-  HAVE-BEEN-FRIGHTENED-OF-YOU-PIECE–OF-SHIT"!! he screamed at me.

`I'm definitely going to give this man a heart

attack I thought`. Holding back the laughter I carried on. "Sir"….(big pause)…..''It was then that I ushered my girl into the WRNS quarters only to find absolute mayhem going on inside, what with the screams and all that. Whilst in a corridor, she spotted Annie Gaff, sorry Chief Wren Gaff coming our way, so she directed me into the toilets to hide until all the commotion had died down whereupon I would just walk out and back to my accommodation, the rest you know about. Sir".

(It rolled off my tongue like pure sweetness!).

Already knowing that's exactly what my lass had said to him earlier. Head in his hands whilst sat down behind his desk I could see that he had to accept my story….it was so convincing. A minute of silence went by not a word spoken………

"FUCK OFF Ditch, Get-out-of-my- FUCKING SIGHT!! He yelled. I was out of his office in a flash, all his Regulating Staff giving me the evil eye as I walked through the main entrance as they had heard every word…I just smiled and wished them a "Good morning".

A couple of days later and I was again summoned to see the Joss-man!

"Mr. Ditch, it has occurred to me that your uniform appearance is not up to standard as I have watched you walk past my office, so with that I am giving you 3 days notice to get your kit ready for a muster. Okay"? And with that, excused me from his office.

`Tosser`. I thought.

Can't get me on anything so he's trying me with my kit. If one thing was spot-on at all times, it was my appearance!! My kit was laid out immaculately for his muster and there I was stood to attention in front of it. In he walks, 5 seconds into it,

"Where's your gas mask then Slippery"? With a look of `Got you now` splattered all over his face!

I could feel myself clutching at straws!!

"Isn't it there Sir? I must have left it with my detachment kit up at the Squadron" was my hesitant reply.

"Well fuck-me, someone doesn't like you Mr. Ditch because this was found yesterday in one of the WRNS toilets" and with that, pulls out my gas mask from a black bag he was holding. He was grinning from ear to ear! So much for having to put a stamped `dog-tag` on your mask with all your details I thought! For once I was stuck for words and decided enough was enough, these fuckers would never give in until they have won and this particular gentleman was determined to nail me once and for all!!

"Eh, yes Sir, that's mine alright" I replied, on inspecting the dog-tag. The joss-man turned around in my room and walked straight out, chuckling to himself.

I was so pleased for him as the man was on the verge of a nervous breakdown, no honestly I was.

It was probably affecting his family life after work as well. I could imagine him talking to his missus about me whilst eating his cottage pie and veg! Hahahahaaha!

Oh well I thought, `you've had a good run and now you have to face the music Ditchy boy`!

5 or 6 weeks went by where virtually every other day, names would be read out over the Establishments tanoy system for certain individuals to report to the Regulating Office. Trying to swap as much info` as possible with whoever was in before you, just before you were summoned in for a roasting. Give the Regulating Staff their due though, they worked round the clock preparing

119

statements, questioning, doubling back over and over.

"Who murdered who?" we would ask one another. These guys were hell bent in doing us all and with that said that the rest of the camp would `Fall in line`, or so they thought!

One of the Joss-mans female staff whilst questioning me thought she would go down the "Are you a homosexual?" route. It was Instant dismissal from the service if you dabbled down that street! I just looked at her across the interview table as though to say `I would probably rather turn homo than bed you darling`…she was not the prettiest of females, bless her!

The Air base around the late 70`s to mid 80`s was buzzing. You had rivalry between the Commando Squadrons, between the Writers and the Chefs, almost every different trade. The camp by no means was as bad as some of the shit you read about these days in newspapers, about guys being bullied to the extent where upon they commit suicide!

Now that would have put the Joss-man in a straight jacket!! With all his paperwork prepared the Joss-man and his team gave us all a date for our come-uppance in front of the Commander! On that day of judgement, the front of the Guardroom looked like a queue at a taxi rank on a Saturday night. 32 of us had been hauled forward to face the music! 6 of them were Wrens! 1 of them, the girl who had lied for me! She was to get off the lightest with £100 fine. This was 1982 remember and £100 went a long way! The rest of the punishments went from her fine up to around £500 along with numerous No.9s and No.10s (extra work mainly in the kitchens, extra mustering, kit inspections, sleeping in the guardroom, drill, etc).

The 9s and 10s ranged from 14 days to 90 days!! Titch got tossed outside. He had already had a spell in DQ`s. I got 28 days Detention Quarters in Pompey Dockyard (but actually only did 21 because I just kept my head down and got on with it and so was given 1 weeks remission). Jez got 90 days (second class for conduct).

After we all received our various punishments the Joss-man and his team went for a piss-up to celebrate all their hard work, to this day, I and others believe that they probably had 4 of our so-called `mates` with them, pissing-up as well. Funny how they were in the thick of everything and then come the day, they walked Scott free!!! You know who you are!

Hey, I bare no grievance or grudges....but it must be a shit feeling for you because I know that you all still reminisce about the so called……. `good old days`!!

Anyway, off to D.Q`s to do my bit for the Queen!

"Nice haircut son, sit yourself down here" smiled the D.Q`s barber. Within seconds, he had wrapped a bed sheet around my neck, shaved me like Kojak and whipped the sheet back off me! I had fucking welts across my scull where he had dug in!

"NEXT" he bawled at my fellow in-mates whom some of looked very sheepishly.

I Picked up my kit and was shown the way to my ROOM.

`Fucking ROOM`? I questioned.

"That's a CELL if ever I've seen one"! I argued to my escort!

"From now until you leave, that's a fucking ROOM!!

121

He replied and at that shouted "FINGERS"……. and slammed the heavy metal door in my face!

"Hello room"

Room is about 7 foot x 9 foot.
1 x wooden bed.
1 x pillow.
2 x sheets.
2 x blankets.
1 x table.
1 x chair.
1 x window (8 feet up the wall+bars and very small).
1 x Bible.
1 x Ships book. (Training manual throughout RN).

"Hello room"…………… and got my head down for the rest of the day and night! For I would see no-one until tomorrow.

Tomorrow came and I was put in front of the Detention Quarters Commander. He lectured me on everything that he reckoned he knew about me, he lectured me on HIS (not the Royal Navy's ways), he lectured me on lectures and quiet frankly I wasn't listening to a single word!!!

My mind was only on `How many days I had left in this shit-hole! And what was I doing in here?

Fuck me!!!

The fella occupying the ROOM next to me had stabbed his Chief in the neck with a Marlin Spike!!!…. and I was supposed to be a bad lad!! Back to my ROOM for another 24 hours!

I'm bored!

Got to be more to it than this` I thought.

My thoughts were soon answered the next morning at 05:30 sharp! "Front and centre in your doorway, 2 minutes, running kit"! Came an order loud enough to wake the dead! The doors were opened, banging in succession one after the other. I stood just inside it looking out at what you could describe as a fucking big chicken hutch! I was on the upper landing opposite the same amount of ROOMS. Down below the wire mesh than spanned the full width and length of the Quarters was the same amount of ROOMS. It very much resembled the TV programme `Porridge with Ronnie Barker`!

"Left and right turn..........NOW- FUCKING-GET- DOWN- HERE"!!!

As we were being farmed out into a freezing courtyard I turned to one lad and asked him how long you usually run for…His answer was un-fucking-believable!!!

"Until the instructors think that the breakfast is of a reasonable eating standard" he replied.

"YOU FUCKING WHAT"? I said totally confused.

"No fucking chefs in here mate, he said. All of us have to take it in turns to cook all the meals and some guys in here can't boil water so prepare yourself for a good run"!!

Amazing! Absolutely- fucking- amazing!

Hence the ruling that `If 1 fucks up…You all get punished until the 1 gets it right! We ran that morning around the perimeter of the detention quarters, (inside the wall and barbed wire of course) for about 1 and a half hours, with circuit exercises thrown in along the way.

This was all conducted by the Chief Physical Training Instructor, a big imposing man! Who took no shit from no-one, which I picked upon very quickly! Showered up and sat at breakfast, we were not allowed to talk until everyone had finished eating; it was like being in a Monastery!

The lad was right, breakfast was barely edible and I mean barely! "You've got 5 minutes then outside", Said an instructor. I soon got the jest on how this place was run........which made me even more determined to keep my gob shut, do my time and fuck off out of here!

All the instructors apart from the Chief PTI were well past pension age as far as the Services was concerned. They had all done their time but were there basically to top up their service pensions. The worst part of all was that whenever you addressed them whether it is to ask a question or to be spoken to, they would not even acknowledge that you were even stood in front of them until you were as upright and stood to attention as the best fucking Guardsman on Queens Parade!!!

And address them all as SIR!

"SIR"?

Not one of them held a commission;

They were just old and bold senior rates from all services!!

That really got to me but I just looked straight through them when being addressed! Most of the day would be spent sat in a classroom environment having to listen to lectures, mostly about Naval Traditions. Some of the lectures involved practical instruction as well, whereupon things sort of became light hearted and inmates were taking an interest.  Lunch came and lunch went.

More lectures.

"Right that's it for today gentlemen, you have 10 minutes to get up to your ROOMS and back inside the gym where the Chief PTI waits for you" he said with a sadistic look on his face!

This I was looking forward to, as I was intending to go and run for the Fleet Air Arm Field Gun Crew again having ran in 1979, 1 year after I initially joined the RN. You were allowed to go back and run every 3 years if selected., it was now April 82 I'll use this as a starting point to my training leading up to the eliminations I thought.  As expected, the gym workout was intense and seemed to last for hours!  We were infact in there for only 45 minutes but the session was brilliant!!

I really enjoyed that.

After a few more late afternoon sessions, I asked the Chief PTI if he would like to do a weights session every other night and to my astonishment he says, "yeah okay". I was given an extra hours grace at night to take my days frustration out in the weights room with the Chief!!

Alan Price who would become 1st Trainer of the coming years Gun Crew had already spoken to me and said for me to `keep my nose clean` and use DQs to my advantage, of which I did.  I had become focused and worked hard whilst I had my little holiday away.

I was later to find out that when I returned to Yeovilton the Commander informed me that Field Gun was a privileged draft and I was not classed as a privileged person!  So no Gun Crew for me.  Talk about moving the goal posts.  I tried to reason with the Commander that I had done my punishment with good report.  He just gave me some sort of arrogant look as though to say…Tough!! `Yeah, lots of respect for you as well….you tosser` I thought, why am I fucking bothering! Every single day was of the same routine. run,shower,breakfast,lectures,clean,lunch,clean,lectures,P.T. shower, dinner, half hour free time,clean,rounds inspection of ROOMS, fingers!!Doors, out-lights. Day in-day out!

We were to have a two day lecture on Obesity and Alcoholism! Sat in the classroom, there were jars with pickled human livers inside them and medical things of that nature…to shock us I suppose! All of a sudden, the door opens and in walks the most over-weight, blood-shot eyed person I have ever come across!

This Petty Officer Medic was to give US a lecture; he would have got more response if he had spoken into a mirror! After lunch times he would restart were we left off, the only difference was, was that he had sunk about half a dozen pints in the mess for HIS lunch!!!!!...... Fucking Farce!

Time was banging away and I had literally a few days to go. Had been granted my 1 weeks remission from the Commander who knew everything about me (not)! My plan had worked though, to get out of here as quick as I came in and I was pleased with the way it was going. Saturday mornings was when you were let out. Down to Pompey train station with your duty travel warrant back to your base or ship, having had the statuary brief that IF within 24 hours of leaving you are found to be committing an offence, you would be straight back in for another stint, no questions asked! So there I was brushing the leaves and dirt around the main entrance when this dithering old Chief comes out of his gatehouse and unlocks to let the Provost van in. Out gets a couple of new joiners and waiting to get in was two lads, smiling like Cheshire cats as they were on there way out. I watched while leaning on my brush as the van departed with the two lads giving the dithering old Chief the `finger` out of the back windows with a lot of venom intended. It took him about 2 minutes to do all the fucking locks and then ambled back into his gatehouse and picked up the phone.

"Main gate? Send that fucking van back here now"!!

I nearly crumpled up when he opened up the doors again and there was `pinky and perky` in the back crying their fucking eyes out!!!! Hahahahahaha! Fucking Brilliant!!

"You two are obviously missing us already, now get the fuck back in" he ordered. They trudged back to the main quarters absolutely gutted!!! My time had come to leave and I had no intention of making the same fuck-up as `pinky & perky`! I got my travel warrant, left for the train station and never once looked back.

On getting back to Yeovilton, I reported to the guardroom only to be greeted by the last person on earth I wanted to see.........The Joss-man. He stood on the steps of the guardroom, put out his hand with a...

"Well done Mr. Ditch heard some good reports about you". Was I fucking dreaming this shit or what?

Here I am, 5:30 on a Saturday afternoon being welcomed back by the very bloke who put me away not 3 weeks ago....... (It may not sound long, but I WOULDN'T recommend it to anyone).

We stood for what seemed like minutes but had been seconds, looking at one-another.

"I must have done well for you to be standing here on

a Saturday, what's the catch Sir"?

"No catch at all Ditchy, just though I would show my face and let you know that I'm staying on camp this week-end and will be in the juniors bar tonight for a few beers should you and the rest of your motley crew want to join me" he said as though we were best fucking buddies!!!!!!  Now I really WAS stuck for words!!!

"Erm, erm, tut, erm"…I didn't know what to fucking say!

I was fucking gob-smacked!!

"Erm, yeah okay, I'll be over later on I suppose Sir".

I was totally caught on the back foot and stunned!

"See you all later then Ditchy" and off he went.

Turning round within 4 or 5 steps he says,

"By the way Ditchy, its Saturday night so the names Bill, okay"?

You could have knocked me over with a fucking feather!  I just stood there watching him cross the road thinking` What is this guy up to? Does he really love playing mind games with me`?

I was about to find out later, no doubt.

After I had sorted my gear out and had a shower I looked around for some of the lads but it was like a fucking ghost town in the block so I scrabbled up what coins I had in my locker and proceeded over to the bar. As I went through the foyer I could see about 10 of them sat there with a table full of beer!!

Fucking Happy Days, I thought.

Needless to say, I sat down with them and was brought up to date with what had been going on. "Check this out" said Ali.  "The Joss-man is only wanting to have a beer with us in here tonight, he collared us today and organized it, I recon he's fucking up to something"!!

"Oh really, well check this, He was only standing at the guardroom waiting for me and shook my hand and said I had to call him Bill". I said in disbelief!!!

"Anyway, what the fuck happened to you Stuart? I was whisked off that quick I didn't get to find out what you ended up with".

**"They only sent me on a `drying oot` course didn't the. 8 days with some reet loonies! And the best was, was that I was shown how ta make fuckin frogs by stickin sea shells t`gether and then paintin them green when they were dried!! Day in, day oot man!!!!! And another thing....... even betta, they used to let us oot at neet to gan to the boozers as long as we were back by 11.....fuckin piss-take man!!!!!!! But am cured now man".**

We all fell about laughing kit-bags!!

Stuart had a way of explaining things....the lad should have been a comedian! Jez had now come in from the Automat and was obviously pissed off to see us boozing while he was still doing his puns`. He still had about 70 days to go!!!!!!!! My punishment was a short sharp shock..... His was more of a long slow trudge!! But the Joss-man said he was allowed to join us if he wanted. He came to see what he had in store for us!! It wasn't long after when Bill Mason (the Joss`) came in. The place was relatively empty as it was Saturday night and we sat in a corner far away from the door. Spotting us he walked straight over and counted the beers on the table...

"That will be 11 beers and an orange juice for you eh Jez"? He said. "Well, I thought I might have 1 beer" replied Jez, well knowing that he was on stoppage during his puns`!

"Okay then, just the 1" replied the Joss` and off he went to the bar.

I have never seen a bunch of so called `reprobates` stuck for words as we were at that moment. He even brought the fucking lot over himself in about 3 trips to the bar!!!!

**"There's fuckin something up here. I'm tellin ya man, its not reet man"! "Watch wot ya fuckin sayin when he comes back"** Sounded Stu.

Well actually, there was fuck all up......if anything, as the beer flowed, the more relaxed everyone became. The Joss` actually wanted to clear some bad feelings that we had against him and his team.

"Take it on the chin lads, you played the game and had a long innings but got caught out in the end, remember, we were only doing our job"! He said while looking around the table.

**"I haway man, fuck it, life's too short man.............All reet Bill, you've got my hand, I'll be a gud lad from now on.......Now get the fuckin beers in then"** Stuart said while putting his hand over the table towards the Joss`.

The whole table erupted in laughter, even the Joss`!!!

The rest of the night until closing time was spent going over where him and his team fucked up and how some people would say we had `got away with blue murder`...........
Like the Joss` said........................

We Played The Game!!!

# THE PINACOLADA
# REGATTA

In 81` part of the Squadron embarked onto HMS Hermes with a couple of cabs and we were off to the States!! Having spent time at an Air station in Jacksonville, we moved on to North Carolina and did various things with the USMC. Before we left Jacksonville though, we decided to wash our helicopters and enquired with our American friends to what strength and mix ratio should we use there cleaning fluid. Having been given the necessary information, we got about cleaning our cabs. All was going well and the guys who were not cleaning got about packing up our bits n bobs ready for us to fly back onboard to then sail for N.Carolina.

Having now got immaculate looking helicopters we passed the foam cleaning equipment onto the `Pinger` cabs that were with us. The Pingers are painted blue and are Anti-submarine helicopters and even though we were all of one uniform, the squadrons kept themselves to themselves as each thought and still do to this day, that they are better than one another! "What's the mix for this gear then?" One guy asks. "10:1 ratio mate" said one of our fellas. "Yeh, ok, you wanker, you must think we are all thick, eh?" "We'll do it 6:1......tosser"!! Once again, we find ourselves laughing kit-bags as we are taking off in our cabs watching the Pingers trying like merry hell to wipe this cleaning fluid off there cabs as they witness the blue paint turning into blue watery streaks....all the way down the cabs!! Hehehehehe!!......the ratio was actually 2:1 hehehehe!!

Comical.


North Carolina came and went and a great time was had by all. We were now sailing south towards the Virgin Islands. The ship was to sail to St. Thomas and around 12 of us boarded two of our cabs and flew off for 12 days for so called `mountain flying` on the island of Tortola.

Tortola was and is the stuff that lottery money buys you.

Turquoise waters, beach coves lined with palm trees and a really laid back Caribbean feel to the place. In the time we were there the aircrew achieved their mountain flying training and we made the most of Tortola during our time off! Brian Southard was the detachment Senior Maintenance Rating and was an `old salt` himself. He and the other old and bold Senior Rates would sit in the doorway of their tent and spin dits into the early hours whilst sipping away at copious amounts of Pussers Rum!!

Unbeknown to us Junior and not so well travelled matelots, Tortola is the place where Pussers Rum is distilled and the factory was on the other side of the island. Early into the detachment, Brian and his cronies had visited the factory for a tour and had come away with a case of the precious liquid!

"Any chance of a slug of that Chief before we hit town?" I ask.

The old & bold had been organizing this part of the whole trip back in England before we left and were all set up in the Caribbean with their `Chefs cooking pot full of Rum`.

"Crack-on" said Brian in a sadistic sort of way.

Using a plastic field mug (which , by the way holds 1 pint of liquid), I began to push away the scum that had grown on top of the precious liquid which was in the chefs cooking fanny and then filled my mug to the brim. Within two big mouthfuls of the said liquid, I was emptying my mug contents back into the `fanny` and started to experience the wall of fire dancing around inside my mouth whilst feeling the pain of what felt like an axe in my chest!

"JESUS!!!!!!"……

I had never experienced anything like it and here was these old farts sat around this pot as though they were guarding the crown jewels!!! Sipping away at it and grinning from ear to ear.

"Welcome to the Royal Navy" quipped Brian while his fellow mates were laughing kit-bags at the faces I was now pulling. I said, sat in the doorway of there tent because that's all we had.

The ships programme did not have Tortola in it and it was a squadron decision to fly off the ship whilst it went on its way and so we had to be self sufficient, so we took 12 man tents ashore with us. These were pitched in between palm trees about 20 meters from the turquoise water which was lapping onto the golden soft sands. Our daily wash was one made in heaven as we simply walked into our very own secluded Caribbean bay, soap in one hand and without a care in the world!! So, anyway. Having left our seniors to carry on with there sea shanties, we made off into town.

Happily named, Roadtown.

This is where we came across an American fella who informs us that he is chartering his boss's yacht and that he is looking for a crew to help him sail it in the annual `Pina Colada Regatta` yacht race which is happening in two days time!! He has decided to enter whilst he is waiting for his next bunch of rich holiday toffs who are renting the yacht and will be sailing around the islands.

"Absolutely no problem" I said trying to contain my excitement. "How many do you need?"

"Oh 5 should be enough" he replied and at that I was off to round up the crew. When he knew that we were in Her Majesties Royal Navy he thought that he had the race sown up and indeed he would have had we all been proficient sailors but alas, we were Aircraft Engineers!! Matter not, we were to sail the yacht with him that coming weekend!

Having gone back to our camp site and spoken with Brian who has said its ok and that we need to let him know who's going and to which island we shall be sailing to so that one of our cabs can come and land on the beach the following day and pick us up. Name and position of island passed on to Brian, myself, knoppy, shiner, chalky and 1 other whose name for this dit will be.......Rupert (don't want to drop him in the shit!!) proceeded down to the jetty in Roadtown where we met up with our skipper.

I will explain now that Chalky was an Army Sergeant

who was attached to our squadron and whose job it was to look after the squadron vehicles, a bloody good diesel mechanic he was as well.

He was also single and had a bank account in Canada (which will become apparent later).

All the yacht skippers were knelt down on the jetty in one long line with their thumbs tied together with string behind their back. The claxon horn sounded and the skippers were fed a large glass of Pina Colada. Once drank, thumbs were released and the crews would bolt down the jetty jumping onto their respective yachts and off they went. Our yacht was named the `Jeannie C` and was about 70 foot long. A beautiful thing with all manner of boys- toys onboard…it really was something else!! The race was on and it wasn't long before this land-lubbing crew knew what they were supposed to be doing!

During the race we were passed down one side by an all female crew whose clothing consisted of just bikini bottoms!!! With their nipples painted red for port and green for starboard they certainly got a lot of attention! We began to exchange various sea ammunition in the form of water bombs and flour bombs whilst filling our bravado with numerous bottles of ale! We soon realized that our yacht was not performing in the race as well as others and we were finding it difficult making the most of the light breeze that was around us. More competent crews were using the breeze correctly and began to leave us behind….that is until Rupert said that he was going to call for back up.

"What the fuck are you on about Rupert" I asked.

"Just watch this matey…just watch this!!"

And with that went down into the cabin area and

proceeded to switch through the channels on the yachts radio system.

"845,845. This is the Jeannie C calling any 845 helicopter in the area" squawed Rupert.

"845 any 845 helicopters, this is the yacht `Jeannie C` calling. Come in 845".

At that, one of our cabs that was already up flying around came back with....

"Jeannie C, Jeannie C, this is Yankee Bravo 845, have you got a problem?"

"You could say that YB, we require assistance if at all possible, we require wind power in our sails and we are wearing the number 16 in red on our main sail, Can you assist 845?" Requests Rupert.

I kid you not.......in less than 1 minute one of our cabs (YB) came hurtling over a mountain top down to where the race was going on. We waved frantically and they soon spotted us and came around behind our yacht. Rupert was still on the radio requesting that they tilt the helicopter main rotors and fill our sails with much needed air!! This soon came in abundance and we were off and running now....laughing kit-bags as we overtook nearly everyone.

The cab after a while then departed to a chorus of...

"Thank you 845 thank you" over the radio!!

Priceless!

It was now that all the other yachts knew that our yacht was being crewed by navy guys and that we were in for some serious attention when we reached our final destination which was an island about another 40 minutes sailing away.

We had been sailing for about 1 and a half hours and the race was over. All the yachts were anchored in this secluded bay which was about 30 in number.

The sight was unbelievable.

Everyone partying and going from yacht to yacht in the little dinghies that each one carried. It wasn't long before everyone wanted to meet the navy boys and we became very popular very quickly indeed.

Rupert was enjoying himself in the company of others with our skipper down in the luxurious cabin whilst washing his tonsils with expensive champagne! Our skipper decided he fancied a smoke (smoke being the kind filled with some sort of hallucinating ingredients!)

Rupert emerged sometime later from the cabin area having sat happily conversing with his new found audience having breathed in the smoke which had now filled the cabin and resembled a back street bar in Hamburg!

His eyes were like organ stops and he again was laughing kit-bags uncontrollably!!

"Great idea….lets get the spinnaker sail rigged up with a bosons chair" he suggested.

He would sit on the make shift rope chair which was attached to the bottom of the sail and then as the sail filled with air we would slowly let out the sail on a line that we were holding.

"Come on, lets fly matey" he shouted as the sail filled and he proceeded up into the blue Caribbean sky. Hollowing and whooping he began to soar upwards swinging on the seat as he went.

"Higher, higher"….requested our new American friends.

"Higher, higher" Rupert was certainly enjoying himself and without a care in the world!!!

From about 50 feet, Rupert decides he is going to do a backward roll off the seat and perform some sort of Olympic diver's routine down into the lush waters below him!  Fuck-me….he hit that water like a brick!!!  We stood on the yacht, and as usual, laughing kit-bags at his miss-fortune!  Rupert emerged from the depths below to rapturous applause from us all……thank god his mind was on another planet…I don't even think he knew what he had just done!

As time went on we were introducing ourselves to all the other yachties and people were starting to load up their dinghies with all manor of ale and the like to take ashore onto the beach where that night was to hold the annual regatta beach party!!

Fuck me this just gets better and better we thought!

"OK yacht crews, everyone ashore for the beach party" came this voice through a loud hailer from a guy stood on the beach.  It was like whacky races with everyone in their dinghies racing for the shoreline.  The beach had 2 wooden type rum bars and the centre point was a huge fire with pigs on spits being roasted around the outside of it.  The music was sounding out from the bars and everyone mingled with one another chatting and drinking.

Brilliant!

"Watch ya mate, do ya fancy making a night of it?" came a request my way from some Australian lass.

"Erm…yeh, ok, what have you in mind?" I asked.

"Well, we could go back to your boat if you want and see what happens eh?" she said in this Aussie drawl accent.  By now, we had been at the party for some time and things were really hotting up!!  Couples were at it laid down in the surf between all the moored up dinghies. Dancing, drinking and generally having a great time.

"Yeh, bollocks, come on then, let me just tell the lads incase they are looking for me" I told her.

"Right, Rupert, this is what's happening" and I informed him of what I was about to get up to.

His part was to slide in the hatch which I will leave half open and down onto the cabin bed whereupon we shall offer a 2 for 1 service to our new Australian found love!

On climbing back onto the Jeannie C, My Aussie love has popped to the bathroom. I go and open the sky light hatch in the front cabin and see that Rupert has borrowed a dinghy and is on his way towards us.

"Give us 10 minutes mate and then slither in through the hatch and we will present our request to her, OK?" I instructed Rupert.

"No problem my friend, no problem" he quipped.

So, there I was in all my glory laid on the bed and in walked Miss Australia herself. Without going into too much detail.........the whole bay, not just the boat started to rock!!!!!! As planned, the snake like stealthiest of Rupert started to emerge through the sky light hatch. Whilst performing my duty in the missionary position, my Aussie partner was eyes closed and enjoying the whole deal until that is, when my partner in crime Rupert became stuck half-in-half-out of the said hatch!!

I was nearly deafened by the screams that followed!! The noise was unbelievable as she flung me to one side and on getting up off the bed landed my comrade Rupert with a full blooded punch to his ear!!!

"You bastards!!!!" she yelled

"What the fuck is going on?" to a reply of......

"They say two cocks are better than one you know" Rupert informed her in a posh English accent, whilst still stuck in the hatch.

I was again, laughing kit-bags whilst doubled up on the floor as she proceeded to whack him in the other ear!!!

Smack!!!!!

She left the boat in a hurry scrambling onto one of the tied up dinghies and proceeded back to the party leaving me and `Locktite` laughing our heads off!!!!!

I released Rupert from the said hatch and we re-joined the party people on the beach. Everything was rocking now and everyone's having a ball!!

"Right, that's me mate, I'm off, do you fancy coming?" asks Chalky. "Off where mate?" I ask.

"Off out of here mate, having a great time and I am going to have lots more of it" he quips.

"No, I'm going to hang around a bit mate, you go and enjoy yourself" I says to him.

And at that, he was gone.

Last seen walking in the surf with a gorgeous lass on each arm!!

"Go on Chalky my son, Go on" I shouted.

Morning came and the last drones of party music echoed around the bay. I pulled myself up off the leather seat that ran around the cabin area on the yacht and took a peak at myself in the mirror.

Not a pretty sight!!

The party had gone as expected and everyone had fun times. The rest of the lads were waking and sorting their selves out.

"Just brilliant that eh?" from Rupert.

"Where did Chalky get to then?" asks Shiner.

"Saw him walking off with two lasses, looking like he was in for a good time" I replied.

"Anyway fellas, we better get back onto the beach as the cab will be coming shortly to pick us up" says Rupert.

Having said our goodbyes and thank you to our skipper we set off for the beach hoping that we would all meet up. Everyone turned up apart from Chalky! People were standing on the decks of their yachts' as we were shouting at the top of our voices... "CHALKY, CHALKY". He must have heard us, as our voices were bellowing around the bay, but, no Chalky!

"Hope he isn't shark food" quips Rupert as we all looked at one another with that `Oh Fuck! Look in our eyes.

At that we heard the dulcet tone of our cab whacking towards us and proceeded to land on the beach.

"All here?" asks the aircrewman.

"All but 1, we can't find Chalky, last seen about 3 this morning on the beach".

"Right, get sat down and we will hover around the bay above the boats, he's bound to hear us, keep an eye out for him and when spotted we will hover over him and winch him up" said the aircrewman.

So, off we went, around the bay for about 15 minutes!

"Fuck!! I hope he's alright, I thought to myself.

The decision was made by the crew that Chalky was missing and that we had to get back ASAP and report this fact! The cab hammered back to Tortola airport and shut down. We all went to see the Detachment Commander and briefed him on everything that happened and the fact that Chalky was not to be found. Another search from the air was carried out by both of our cabs and the authorities informed of what has happened. Everyone had had a brilliant time but had now a sour taste to it all as all we could think about was if Chalky had fell overboard and been had by sharks. We were well warned of the shark population, especially at night when they come into shallow bays to feed.

The thought was fucking horrible!

We had about 3 days to go before we would pack everything up and fly from Tortola to rejoin the ship which was to pick us up on its way back from St. Thomas.

As well as being the island police chief, this huge stature of a man was also the islands resident radio DJ.

"Yo there bro and sistas, am wanting yawl to keep look out for a Mr. Sgt Chalky White, if you see da man, you come and tell the police-man, that's Mr. Chalky of da British Navy Helicopters" he bellowed out over the Tortola radio station in his deep Caribbean accent.

Well.......we nearly fucking cried, laughing at this.....you couldn't make this up!!!!!

Needless to say that with all the searching and radio requests, we never did see Chalky again and the people that need to know had been informed and before we knew it the signals were being sent all over the place. We must have been de-briefed about a dozen times to when we last saw Chalky.

<u>6 months later</u>: Back at work and reminiscing about our time away, Monday morning was different in the fact

that virtually every squadron member was rushing in to work with the Sunday newspapers pointing out this Ariel photograph that had been taken from a low flying aircraft in the Caribbean.

"FUCK ME"!!!!!!!!!

It was Chalky!!

There he was waving and surrounded by scantily clad women on this yacht somewhere out there on the ocean!

We could not believe it….Fucking Chalky….you old dog!!

That was definitely the last time we saw Mr. Sgt Chalky White.

Oh, the Canadian bank account? Well, he obviously knew what he was going to do didn't he?

Oh and a good diesel mechanic as well, (yachts have diesel engines). Good luck Chalky!

# FROM YEOVIL TO BOSNIA

`D` Flight had been warned out that we were to take over from another flight in Bosnia.

We got our kit together and anything else that we thought would make life a little more comfortable.

Block 4 had been given to the squadron in a shit state!

Whilst everyone else (Dutch, French, German, Army, RAF) had feathered their own nests, we, the Navy squadron was given this totally run down place in one corner of the camp. Farthest away from our work and more importantly, the dining hall! As time went by, each flight started to do bits n bobs around the block and if anything around the camp was not secure or tied down, then we had it! It wasn't long before we had stuff like light bulbs, shower heads, air con units and paint to brighten the place up.

The lads, Senior Rates and Officers all had their own bars within the block and each ran theirs accordingly. Any goings on within the bars was to be kept within the bars and sorted out…best way!

Over a period of time block 4 was starting to be

talked about around the camp and it wasn't long before we had visitors. Each weekend (work and weather permitting) would be taken up with some sort of themed party in the back garden area. This became a popular thing throughout the camp and before we knew it we were having Christmas parties in the middle of summer!!! Great fancy dress as usual (where do these guys get the kit from? I'm sure people must have packed it in their bags to take out there!).

The squadron was making a name for itself in Bosnia as the Aircrew were battling against all weather (not forgetting the shit that was being thrown up at them from the dick-heads on the ground!) to re-supply the lads in more vulnerable areas. The cabs also played a vital role in Casualty Evacuation. It was definitely a case of `work hard-play hard`. We kept ourselves to ourselves and life wasn't too bad.

80s punk rock band, `The Stranglers` along with other supporting acts were to visit Bosnia and do a Forces show...............Who's got the most accessible hanger in Bosnia?

We have!

So, it was a case of getting a stage built with the entire lighting etc for this show.

Show time came and all the acts were brilliant!

Everyone that could be spared was spared and bus loads of guys and girls came to our camp. Beer was allowed during the show and people were just generally enjoying themselves. We got wind that `The Stranglers` were invited back to the Army Seniors bar after the show and that all other senior ranks were also invited. Jet Black, the drummer of the band turned to us and said..

"Fuck me! Whose funeral is it?"

He was commenting on the fact that the Army bar was like a fucking morgue!

"Thought you lot liked a good piss up now and again?" He said.

"Mate, this is the Army and that guy stood over there is the dad of the pad" said one of our lot as he pointed to the Mess RSM stood playing with the ends of his moustache.

"You are not going to get a party going in here that's for sure" I said  but I know somewhere where you will and with that I had a word with my boss and the invites were now on!!!  Bob and I ran ahead to get the bar open and to make sure our fridges were fully loaded!  Everything was tickety-boo and ready for our guests…

"We'll show them how to party" said Bob. And with that the door bursts open and its full steam ahead!

Within minutes our bar was packed and a good night awaited us.  "Hold on everyone hold on, we aint got any change behind the bar and we aint doing chits tonight" Shouted Mac.

"So I want all the change you have over this bar now" he carried on.  At that, the Manager of The Stranglers came forward and presented himself to me, Bob and Mac behind the bar.

"Will this do for you lads" he said and opened up the tour briefcase and placed a wad of notes on the bar top.

"Give me a shout when that runs out" he said as Bob cranked the music up and Mac stood on the bar top shouting "Let's get ready to party!!" The rest of the night went brilliantly until our Army friends decided they would invite themselves as they have heard that we have the dancing girls from the show earlier on now dancing for us on our bar top! Oh, and by the way, they are all dressed in red PVC uniforms…and yes they had very short skirts as well!!! I got wind of this and decided to make sure that if they wanted in then they played by our rules and with that I positioned myself outside the bar entrance with a desert spoon in one hand and a bottle of vodka in the other.

"Now then my friends, entrance to this bar is via the vodka spoon of which you will snort dry through a nostril of your choice" I informed them as they walked up the corridor towards me.

"And if you cheat or decline to do it then its back to your morgue for you lot".

We couldn't believe what we were seeing;

there you have about a dozen guys queuing up as if they were in a doctor's surgery waiting to meet with the vodka spoon!!

"Are these all fucking thick or what "asks Bob.

When snorted, their eyes were streaming and they just looked on in the queue as though they really had to do this hahahahaha!

Soon after, we had a visit from the Army females who wanted in on the Stranglers Party.

"Now then girls, have I got a surprise for you, entrance to our bar is gained by eating 2 pickled gurkins of which I have a jar full" I informed them. These were not just any pickled gurkins;

these were from the market in town and were as hot as hell and about 3 inches long and as thick as a sausage!

"So, roll up-roll up, who's first?"

"You are mate, gone on you do it, go on, dare ya?" came a request from one of the lasses.

"Go on, double dare ya" said another.

These gurkin things were not to be taken lightly and everyone on the camp knew of them! "Go on, double-double dare ya" said another.

Bob looked at me as though to say `you going to do it or what mate? Think of the piss take that will happen if you don't?` Now, anyone who knows me knows that I would rather eat grass than eat gurkins!!

I can't stand the rancid things!!

The girls stood there waiting to see what the reply would be...... Bob looked on with a look of hope that I was not going to let my fellow brothers down!

"Come on then, but I have to spice them up a bit first" and at that the girls were hollowing in frenzy!

The look on Bobs face said it all. `How the fuck can you **spice** them up?` With that I spun around and whipped down my jeans and without any pants on... whistled one of these beauties up my arse!!

I don't know whether they were shocked or the screams were screams of laughter but they retreated down the corridor to a safer distance. Having held the foreign bodied object inside me for about 10 seconds, I urged it out into my hand, spun around and popped it straight into my gob!!!

Now I did have them screaming!!

"NEVER-EVER-EVER... dare- a- darer" I shouted as they scrambled for the main door!

"Well Bob, that's the last we will see of them I recon" I said as I stood on a seat to throw up out of the nearest window!

Now, had the girls been half decent then the entrance

issue wouldn't have been a problem but these were old school Army hoppers!!!!

They say that beauty is skin deep, well this lot must have been born inside out!!

With that over we went back into the bar which was now rocking! Time went on and at around 4 in the morning the tour manager was now with an empty briefcase and decided that it was time to leave and phoned the bus driver to come pick them up. Bob has now become friends with `the stranglers` and we say our goodbyes inside the bar but not Bob, he has to see them to their tour bus outside. Virtually all the guys in the block have got their heads down now and the place is relevantly quiet. Bob escorts our visitors down stairs and opens the front door for them. They get on their bus that is waiting for them outside the block and as soon as they are sat down began pissing themselves with laughter as there is Bob dancing like a mad man at the bus side, pissed out of his head whilst blowing a whistle........Its 4 in the morning remember. Unbeknown to Bob, stood behind him in his slippers and dressing gown was the squadron Engineering Officer and very pissed off he was looking too! Bob was oblivious to this and danced more like a demonic tribal witch doctor!

The bus departed with Bob shouting his goodbyes at them.

"Fuck-me, what a good night Bobbie boy hey, what a good night" Bob slurred to himself as he turned to walk back into block 4.

"It is not as good as what the morning is going to bring `Bobbie boy`, do- you -know -what- the- fucking-time- is? See you in a couple of hours....... PETTY

OFFICER!!!! The AEO had been woken from his beauty sleep!

Oh shit!!!

# A FRIDGE FULL
# OF LOO ROLL!

Our bar in Bosnia had been closing at the latest, midnight, for a while now. We didn't want to ruffle the feathers of the AEO any more than we had to and Bob had used up the detachments worth. And so the time was rolling on and it was soon that our flight would be getting relieved by another. With a couple of weeks to go before we return home, `Topsy` Turner was given 48hrs compassionate leave and so made his way to the airport to be flown home.

"Hey, hold on Topsy, I'm going to go round the lads and get them to cough up some dosh and you can bring some Indian Takeaway back for us?" Suggested Jack.

"Christ!! Id kill for a curry...Here's a tenner mate and I'll have anything" I said excitedly.

"Here's my £10 Jack, and mine, heres mine Jack, mine as well, as the lads were throwing money at him, it just went on and on and on! In the end, Jack had about £200 in his hand and went to brief Topsy on what we would like.

"I can't wait to see how he's going to carry all that back here" says Bob. "Don't worry yourself, I have a plan!" replied Topsy, and with that, he was off back to the UK to do whatever he had to do. We had two days to organize our bar so a couple of fellas went to the market down town to root through and lay their hands on some Indian music. Others scoured the camp for any microwave ovens that were loafing around while the rest of us decorated the bar appropriately and sent out the necessary VIP invites so we could have ourselves a good night when and more importantly, if, Topsy returned with said Indian cuisine at hand!

"I wont believe it till I see it, said Mac, the crabs aren't gonna carry that back here, no fucking way!" 48hrs later... low and behold............Topsy is outside block 4 with the crabs (RAF) doing all the donkey work for him!

"You haven't?" said Bob, shocked.

"I fucking have!" replied Topsy

"Wait and see what I have in here" whilst pointing to a `Thomas-bin` covered in masking tape with things written like...

GIRO, HANDLE LIKE EGGS and AIRCRAFT COMPONENTS, VERY FRAGILE and THIS WAY UP ONLY.

How they never smelt the gear inside is a miracle!!! Topsy, true to his word when he got home had picked up a Thomas-bin when he arrived back at the squadron in UK. He then went home and sorted what he had to sort. Then the next night, he went to the Viceroy Indian Restaurant in Yeovil and laid £100 in tenners on the bar top.

"This is a deposit, I will be here at 5am tomorrow morning whereupon I will give you another £100 and in return I would like this Thomas-bin filled with your best gear"......and by the way fellas, make it good as it is going out to Bosnia and you could get some advertising out of this" asks Topsy..........The restaurant staff stood there in amazement as they had never had a request like this before.

The trusty Thomas-bin measured about 4`x3` and about 2` deep with a tight fitting lid, green in colour and made of sturdy stuff as we used them a lot when in field exercise conditions for carrying aircraft or domestic equipment. Topsy picked up the bin at 5am and drove his hire car to RAF Lynham where the plane waited to bring another lot of guys out to Bosnia. He had the usual crap of being processed by the `movement's team` (fucking jobs-worth lot!!) and then get his kit onto the plane.

"I'll look after that for you boss" said one of the team as he delegated two of his lads to carry our Thomas-bin onto transport waiting outside. "Watch what you are doing with that, you dicks, don't you know how fragile that stuff is!" he yelled at his two youngsters.

`Thomas the bin` was taken on his own transport to the waiting aircraft and given a gentle lift onboard...not thrown on like all the other bits! Topsy stood there in awe of all this!!

A couple of hours later and Topsy is stepping off the aircraft back into the warmth of the afternoon breeze on the dispersal at Split airport, Bosnia.....with Thomas the bin!!! And still the crabs hadn't cottoned on! One of our land rovers was there to pick him up but Topsy ushered them away saying that he had his very own transport and at that an RAF land rover pulled up and two guys gently so gently lifted Thomas the bin emblazoned with `handle with care!` signs into the vehicle!

By now we had the bar decorated and with authentic crap Indian restaurant background music coming from the music box. On the bar top sat 8 microwave ovens and the fridges below the bar were brimming with freezing cans of lager!!! Paper plates, knives, forks & spoons were positioned at the start of the microwave line. Our C.O. was on an operation further up country at the time so unfortunately could not be with us for what was going to be a feast extravagance! Bob though was there and agreed to be our VIP for the night…appropriate really as he had been Commanding Officer of our squadron previously and was passing through the area and had decided to visit the lads…Top bloke was Bob!! Thomas the bin was opened in his entire splendour and the contents placed on the tables in front of the bar………….how wonderful those tables looked!!

"Everyone smile then" came the instruction as the cameras started flashing. The Indian Official photograph came out a treat! The cold lagers were being opened and all the lads started to get stuck in…….ping-ping-ping-ping-ping….the fucking microwave ovens were getting a battering as plate after plate of Tandoori, Balti, Tikka masala,Jalfrezi, and other lovely dishes were heated up and then demolished!!! Nan breads, more rice than a paddy field! Bombay potatoes, onion bhaji`s, Vegetable curries, pickles & chutneys, Samosa`s,…..

Fuck-me, we had the LOT!!!!

As the banquet rolled on the lager was flowing well.

"That's one fridge down mate" shouts Bob from behind the bar, "Another three to go! Shall I re-stock it?"

"No mate.............Fill it full of `bog rolls` I think we are going to need something cooling for our arses after this lot!" I replied.

Days went by and our relief date was just around the corner. Topsy had gone home just before us and as a thank you gesture, took an 9x6 photograph of us all crowded around our bounty of food into the Viceroy Restaurant to say...

`Thanks`.

The day we got on the plane to fly home, the Commanding Officers phone was as busy as the Bat Phone in Gotham City! Questions needed answering to why tax payer's money has been spent using RAF aircraft to transport Indian Takeaways from Yeovil to Fucking Bosnia!!!!!!.................... The restaurant photograph had only ended up in the Western Gazette local newspaper hadn't it!

Brilliant!

# CONCLUSION

Well, there you have it. Just a couple of lads having fun, in between some hard work may I add, albeit boisterous fun. This book is only the tip of the iceberg and all you out there who I have not named can `Stand Easy` for now because as you know, there's a whole lot more to write about! Not like today where the young lads have the up-to-date mobile phones, their own TV's and DVD players, being able to buy booze from the Naffi shop and drink legally in their single en-suite cabins with the only thing separating them from the females in the block is a fire door! Earning enough money to buy new boy-racer cars! Zooming home at week-ends to mummy with their dirty washing. Buying houses and all by the age of 20!!!!!!!!!! The way the Services are changing, especially the Royal Navy, it wont be long I'm sure before these young lads can opt out of going to Sea should they want to!

My Sweet Jesus!!, what next? (Watch this space). I will finish by saying that a lot of you probably thought these stories were just full of

Shit!

Well my friends........LIFE itself is full of shit...It just all depends on how you handle it!!


So many memories with so many Quality guys.

Yours Aye....Thank you.

Ian Stanley `George` Ditch.

# ABSENT SHIPMATES

Dave Crabtree

Terry Barrat

Lenny Fairclough

George Hay

Tim Gildea

Don Minter

Steve Critchley

John Quail

Fred Farrand

Paul Dunn

Steve langthorpe

*Rest in Peace*